W.O.W.
factor

52 Thoughts from Thought Leaders

How defining words can define your life

HigherLife Development Services, Inc.
P.O. Box 623307
Oviedo, Florida 32762
(407) 563-4806
www.ahigherlife.com

Printed in the United States of America
10 9 8 7 6 5 4 3 2 1

Gingrasso, Chris
WOW Factor: 52 Thoughts from Thought Leaders about Inspiring Words of the Week

ISBN (Hardback) 978-1-939183-60-6
ISBN (Ebook) 978-1-7332289-3-0

Introduction

Have you ever noticed that how you see things can make all the difference? When we change our perspective, we can change our attitude. Suddenly, what looked like a closed door, a limiting belief, or a dead-end path becomes the passageway to a whole new world.

One minute you feel overwhelmed—and not in a good way—like twenty different voices are all clamoring for your time and attention. It paralyzes you. But then the next minute, you can be just as overwhelmed—but in a good way, like when you stand on the south rim of the Grand Canyon and look out over the majesty of creation. Being overwhelmed like that is awe-inspiring.

The goal of this book is to give you a fresh perspective and some new ways of looking at familiar Words of the Week (WOW) that will pull and provoke you to greatness—that's what I call the "WOW Factor." Listen, I am a very busy sales professional, author, husband, and father. I always want to be as productive as I possibly can be, but to be honest, I struggle to make time to feed myself the mental, emotional, and spiritual nutrients to help me stay the course—to be a great husband, a cool dad, an amazing friend, a trusted leader. Oh yeah, and to crush my sales goals.

I got to thinking about the kinds of things that motivate me, inspire me, and help me find that right perspective so I can be the best version of me I can be. I decided to invite a group of people who, over the years, have helped positively shape my life in one way or another. I wanted to share their passion, their vision, their lives, and even their failures with more people so we can all gain a new perspective and perhaps a better definition of some key life words. This is how *WOW Factor* came to be.

This group of leaders you are about to read and learn from is diverse. Each person I've invited to participate has superstar qualities I believe you will appreciate and learn from. The contributors to this book come from dif-

I

ferent leadership levels, different industries, and very different backgrounds. We also represent different generations: Industrialists, Boomers, GenXers, and Millennials. One thing we all have in common is our sheer determination to live in the *WOW Factor* world. We are learning that defining a word properly can create a whole new path to a more fulfilling life, both at home and at work.

None of these writers is perfect. Far from it. But they are all gifted leaders who are students of life and are still learning. And like you, they are still becoming who they were created to be. This is a group of CEOs, coaches, leadership development specialists, engineers, entrepreneurs, global leaders, branding gurus, sales managers, retired military, performers, and a few ministers—all committed to living, and helping you live, a WoW kind of life!

It is my hope that these words of the week will weave their way into your everyday life—both personally and professionally. It is my desire that this book becomes a small but significant piece of your daily puzzle to simplify your complex life. I want you to examine it. Explore it. "Chew" on it. Share it. And most importantly, *live it*! These narratives are not designed to be exhaustive studies of the meaning of the words themselves, but rather a springboard of creative, meaningful, practical revelations that hopefully will cause you to dig deep into your own soul and cause you to live in the *WOW Factor*.

My suggestion is to go through each WOW (Word of the Week) factor on the first day of your week. Most of us start our workday on Monday. Whatever day starts your week, I dare you to be disciplined enough that every week, you decide, commit, plan, and promise to open your mind and soul to the WOW Factor.

If you learn something from this book, please *share, tell, give, practice,* and *repeat*!

Now…get ready to unlock the WOW Factor.

Chris Gingrasso
General Editor

Table of Contents

"Attitude is the little thing that makes the BIG difference."

– Winston Churchill

ˈadəˌt(y)o͞od

Noun

1. *a settled way of thinking or feeling about someone or something, typically one that is reflected in a person's behavior.*

2. *a position of the body proper to or implying an action or mental state.*

If you know (or ever were) a typical teenager, then you have observed what *attitude* is! You know that look in their eyes, or the flip of their hair… or worse, the roll of their eyes. Sometimes it can just be the way they are standing. Of course, you are trying to be a great person, so you find yourself correcting the teen, and then he or she gives you an "attitude."

But what is it, really? It is actually a little difficult to describe, right? What does a bad attitude look like? What about a good one?

What about in the workplace? Would you hire someone if everyone you asked about this person said, "Oh, he/she has a bad attitude"? What if you had a problem and you called the company that made your product, and the customer service rep had a bad attitude? Even if you liked the product, or service, I suspect, like me, that you would steer away from that company.

What makes an attitude good or bad? Who can determine that presumed reality? An attitude is the way we express ourselves. Look at the prefix of this word, "at"—it means "expressing location or arrival in a particular place or position." So our attitude is our arrival to our position that is expressed. Our attitude is often presented in facial expressions and body language. It is really our inner view coming to the forefront. Like the curtain has been pulled back.

I think we would all agree, no one likes a bad attitude. Thank goodness we all lose this trait after we grow out of the teenage years…yeah, right. Face it, we develop a bad attitude if we are not careful.

So what can cause a bad attitude? I personally think it is mostly how we react when something does not go our way. That is most evident with me in traffic. Have you ever driven in central Florida? It is crazy nuts! Seventy-five percent of people are lost, on their phones, and switching across four lanes of traffic at the absolute last second. Maybe because many of the drivers are from another state, country, or very likely on vacation. It makes for a real mess!

So let's be honest…how do you react when things do not go the way you expect them to? Perhaps, just like when we were teens, you cop a "'tude." Here are four L's that can help you have a better attitude:

Look for the positive. Whatever we look for, we will eventually find. If all we do is look for the negative…we will find that exact thing. The same is true with looking for the positive. There is always something positive we can find.

Listen to motivation (concepts/people). New concepts can be exciting, and people who are leading or developing these concepts are full of hope. People who are fun to hang with, dreamers, optimists, and those who even take risks (the potential thinkers) are the people we need to surround ourselves with. They tend to rub off on us and give us hope.

Leverage what things you can change. Fix what you can fix, but don't bother to point out a problem without at least one possible solution. American poet Maya Angelou once stated, "If you don't like something, change it, but if you can't change it…then change your attitude."

Leave the frustrations/hurts behind. Why carry them around? It will only drag you down. Forgive fast, and walk on. We have all been hurt in this life by a spouse, a child, a mentor, or a boss. (Heck, we've been hurt by society as a whole.) They have let us down. Perhaps they have disappointed us. Hurt us. Does that give us a right to have a bad attitude? No!

Let's be honest, some days are hard. I am in health care and own numerous businesses, and sometimes things do not go as planned—or I should say, as I have planned. With this awareness, I choose to have a positive attitude before I walk into any room. The patients, family members, and others I'm about to interact with deserve my best attitude. So I now make sure that during the last ten minutes of my drive toward my home, especially after a difficult day, I focus on bringing a great attitude home. I work on the four L's *before* I get home.

In his book *7 Reasons Why You Should Have a Positive Attitude,* Ryan Low says, "Having a positive attitude allows you to be more productive at work and around the house. People who have a positive attitude regularly set goals and achieve them…Being able to accomplish things regularly is found in a positive attitude, and it enhances that attitude at the same time."

> *"Weakness of attitude becomes weakness of character."*
>
> **– Albert Einstein**

Attitude is written by Dr. Paul C. Sorchy ll

"I believe your atmosphere and your surroundings create a mind state for you."

– Theophilus London

['atməs,fir]

Noun

1. The envelope of gases surrounding the earth or another planet

2. The pervading tone or mood of a place, situation, or work of art

An *atmosphere* is a surrounding environment or influence. It is not only the protective shield surrounding our planet so we can live, it is also a protective shield protecting our lives. This is true of our homes and also the offices in which we work. For example, if you or your coworkers talk behind each other's backs, you will create a nasty atmosphere at work.

Think about this...some things simply cannot survive when the atmosphere is not compatible with them. In other words, if something is not similar or at least complementary, then it simply cannot exist there.

I remember fishing with my oldest son. We were deep-sea fishing in the Gulf of Mexico when a crazy thing happened. I was reeling in a fish (a mighty *huge* one, of course). When it finally landed in the boat and we were pulling the hook from its mouth, I had the thought that it sure must be a crazy feeling to be that fish when all of a sudden you are about to take a bite of your lunch, and then, in a split second, your whole world changes.

Just then, he (I think it was a boy fish) freaked out and wigged and flapped so much that he bounced off the bottom of the boat, back into the water. Why did this happen? I am guessing, but it might be because that fish was determined to be back in a familiar place. Maybe he instinctively knew he had to get to a place where the atmosphere was right for him if he were to survive.

I wish I were more like fish sometimes. I wish I would fight to stay in a healthy atmosphere. Perhaps too often, we all just sang along with Doris Day when she sang, "Que sera, sera, whatever will be will be…" No! We have the ability, as leaders, to help create the atmosphere we desire. Think about this. If we create an atmosphere of optimism, how can pessimistic people survive there? They will, like the fish, jump out of the boat.

Ask yourself, "What is the atmosphere in the office where I work?" What about the atmosphere of your home? Now that harder question: How have you contributed to the reality you feel?

Have you ever walked into a room and just "felt" something? Maybe you could not even explain it. Was it sad? Was it exciting? What caused that feeling? Perhaps it was an individual or a group of people who created the atmosphere in the room. We actually have the ability to *create* a mood in a room.

For me, this becomes especially important when I come home after traveling for the day of work. I focus on what I can do to bring an atmosphere of peace, joy, and love. And to be honest, I have no idea what I will walk into. You see, after years of providing foster care to teenagers, on any given day, we usually have a few extra children at our house. Combined with my own crazy bunch, and their friends, it can be a circus, as some have described. So what I bring home needs to be the peace, joy, and love I mentioned earlier.

It is the same in the workplace. If you are in an office, what atmosphere do you allow to exist? You might say, "Well, I am not the boss, or the owner," but it does not matter! Each of us has the ability to help create the atmosphere around us. For example. if you do not want gossip to be part of your environment, then nip it as soon as it rears its ugly head!

Following the five E's below can help you create a healthy, positive atmosphere:

1. **Envision** what can be, and do not settle for anything else.

2. **Examine** your heart to see if there's anything you are doing or saying that is negativity contributing to the atmosphere.

3. **Encourage** others to participate in the positive direction and focus.

4. **Embrace** your good feelings.

5. **Enjoy** the atmosphere you helped create.

"Behave so the aroma of your actions
may enhance the general sweetness of the
atmosphere."

– Henry David Thoreau

Atmosphere is written by Chris Gingrasso

"To be authentic, we must cultivate the courage to be imperfect—and vulnerable. We have to believe that we are fundamentally worthy of love and acceptance, just as we are. I've learned that there is no better way to invite more grace, gratitude, and joy into our lives than by mindfully practicing authenticity."

– Brené Brown

/ôˈTHen(t)ik/

Adjective

1. *Of undisputed origin; genuine*

2. *Music (of a church mode) Comprising the notes lying between the principal note or final and the note an octave higher*

Early in my adult life, I was given a painting that no one else in my family claimed. It was done in oil, mostly primary colors, and it depicted a Florida mangrove swamp at sunset. Honestly, it was pretty ugly.

Out of duty, I hung it in my home for a year or two. Then, when I thought others wouldn't notice, I promptly moved it to the basement, where it remained, house to house, move to move. Each time we'd move, I'd unpack it and leave it in the basement. After the last move, I never even unwrapped it.

Fast-forward eighteen years. My neighborhood was having a yard sale, and I decided to unload some "stuff." So I put the picture out there with a $5 tag on it. All was well until I noticed that someone had picked it up and was examining it with a jeweler's loop, paying particular attention to the signature. Fortunately for me, the buyer passed on the purchase, but I retrieved the painting and began an online search about the artist. Long story short, it was painted by someone who had quite a following, the only female in a group called "The Florida Highwaymen." I recently sold it at auction for several thousand dollars. Who knew? Judging by what I saw, there was no value in the painting.

How can we lean in and learn from this example? Being true to oneself has become increasingly difficult to do. When I think about the word *authentic*, I am reminded that being an original, showing value through who I am and how I live, does not always fare well in a society of conformity. The world is watching, looking through that jeweler's loop. Conformity causes each of us—young and old, business leaders and homemakers—to settle for things that define us that are not true to who we are.

If we unpack this, it's pretty compelling. Each one of us is designed for our own measure of greatness; each one of us has a sphere of influence and the opportunity to live a life of dynamic impact. Maybe you have been lucky enough to move into a role where you can set a vision and navigate your life based on how *you* chart the course. We all imagine our lives will be like that, and we all have great aspirations be dynamic forces of change and people of value.

How do you know that's true? Read the aspirations of your classmates from your high school yearbook. Most everyone intended to be a world-changer. It's hard to get to that place as life throws curve balls at us and we find ourselves trying to fit, restrained by the mandate to conform. Our value can be lost as we strive to "fit in" and "not make waves." The truth is, the world *is* looking at us through a jeweler's loop, looking for something that is real. We shy away from the loop, feeling vulnerable and concerned that our flaws will be magnified for all to see, so we hide behind the safe wall of conformity.

Maybe it's time to reunite with the authentic world-changer who faces you in the mirror each morning. You can begin this process by doing the following:

1. Start your day with a pledge to be the honest version of yourself, and earnestly commit to that. Compromise is a way of life, but striving to be authentic will help recenter you each day.

2. Determine each day that you will be fully present, in the moment, and comfortable in your own skin. We miss critical, in-the-moment interactions when our sights are set on what's next.

3. Genuinely strive to impact others with kindness and openness. When you are real and open, others are drawn in and charged to change.

You won't get this exercise down overnight; it takes time and determination. You will fail; the world will try to keep you on the side with the crowd vote. But if you practice this, you will gain ground each day by being authentic, true to yourself, and real. You'll like yourself a lot. And really, you're going to make people smile when they see you coming or when they see you going. The choice is yours. Take the risk, and stay true to who you are. In doing so, remember that we all struggle with the same need for acceptance.

Here are three A's to work on every day:

1. **Affiliate** with others who are honest and fearless; it's galvanizing.

2. **Assess** each life encounter, and decide how to use your "real" voice to add value.

3. **Act.** Start today.

"Be yourself; everyone else is already taken."

– Oscar Wilde

Authentic is written by Donna Bosmeny

"People need to wake up and realize that life doesn't wait for you. If you want something, get up and go after it."

—Robert Kiyosaki

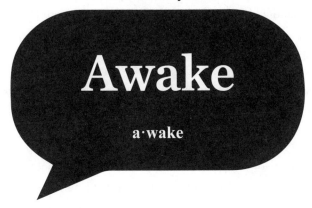

/əˈwāk/

Verb

1. *Stop sleeping; wake from sleep*

Adjective

1. *Not asleep*

I am often guilty of being in a conversation and instead of truly focusing on what the other person is saying, I'm formulating in my head what I'm going to say in response. When I do that, I check out of the moment and am not fully present. I am not fully awake to that conversation anymore. What did I miss?

My full attention would have benefited the person to whom I was engaged in conversation. Or maybe the person who missed out was me. Either way, I lose. It's what happens when we are not fully present…not fully awake to the moment, to the situation at hand.

I was at an outdoor festival recently. It was dusk, and the sun had just set on a beautiful fall Florida evening. A dozen hot-air balloons were tethered to the ground, firing up their gas burners to turn their canopies into giant-sized, colorful light bulbs. The park was lined with vendors and food trucks filling the air with exotic smells to tingle the senses and make you hungry. People were everywhere, walking, talking—the air was electric. Yet in the midst of all this activity, I noticed a young man walking, head down, hands firmly gripping his handheld video game, completely entranced. He was there, he was alive, breathing, even walking. But he was oblivious to what was going on around him.

You've seen this scene before. Video games and text messages, as wonderful as they are, can so captivate our attention that we tune out everything else. It's a technology-induced form of sleepwalking.

There is a time for sleep. As humans, we need it. But outside of the six to eight hours a day we spend doing exactly what our bodies need to recharge, are we guilty of a lesser form of sleepwalking? How can we live our lives being more fully alive, more fully awake to all that is going on around us?

Are there ways you have let the routine of your job, the routine of your marriage, or of life in general cause you to slip into autopilot, to where you are not living fully awake?

You hear soldiers and spies talk about their ability to have a high level of "situational awareness" in any environment be it familiar or new. They have a heightened sense of their surroundings. It's what keeps them alive. But those of us with less exotic professions would benefit from developing our ability to remain fully awake to what's going on around us.

As Whoopie Goldberg famously quoted in her movie *Sister Act*, "If you wanna be somebody, if you wanna go somewhere, you gotta *wake up* and pay attention."

How can you do this? How can you live more fully alive, more awake, to both the people and the opportunities that are before you? It's worth the effort. Here are some thoughts to get you started.

1. **Identify** when you tune out—Chances are, you don't live your whole

day in "slumber mode." But ask yourself, "Where do I tend to 'check out,' even on an unconscious level?" Maybe it's during the routine of answering emails. Maybe you tune out when you get home from an exhausting day at work. Perhaps there are meetings or parts of your job or people who make it easier for you to shift into autopilot.

2. **Get a new perspective**—Take a different route home from work. Look at a problem or circumstance in a new way. Maybe you have a repetitive aspect of your work. Can you turn it into a game, a challenge, or find a secondary goal beyond just getting through the conversation or the task? For example, see if you can make the person who never smiles actually laugh. Make a point to notice something about which you can share a genuine compliment.

3. **Change your routine**—The principle of "muscle memory" is that when you do something over and over in the same manner, the activity becomes routine. For a golf swing, this is a good thing...for a relationship, not so much. *Managers* are paid to maintain the status quo. *Leaders*, on the other hand, are paid to find new opportunities, new paths to higher performance. Leaders need to cultivate the opposite of muscle memory. They need to develop the ability to live awake to "see" opportunities and hidden potential where others don't. But more than just *seeing* what's possible, they have to be willing to *act* on it.

May you live this week more awake than ever before!

"Our truest life is when we are in dreams awake."

– Henry David Thoreau

Awake is written by David W. Welday III

"And, if a beachhead of cooperation may push back the jungle of suspicion, let both sides join in creating a new endeavor—not a new balance of power, but a new world of law—where the strong are just, and the weak secure, and the peace preserved."

– From John F. Kennedy's inaugural speech

/ˈbaləns/

Noun

1. *An even distribution of weight enabling someone or something to remain upright and steady*

2. *A condition in which different elements are equal or in the correct proportions*

Verb

1. *Keep or put (something) in a steady position so that it does not fall*

2. *Offset or compare the value of (one thing) with another*

In life situations, kings, queens, presidents, managers of people, fathers and mothers, and all others in the decision-making process make day-to-day decisions that affect the people under their control. These are our rulers and leaders, in one capacity or another. By definition, there is an expectation that whatever decisions they make are just, equitable, and *balanced*.

However, throughout history, too many times we have seen numerous examples of ruthless leaders who thirst for power and would do anything to preserve this power. They relish and welcome the many perks and benefits that power affords them. They live in expensive homes in exclusive neighborhoods. Meanwhile, the masses of their people live in squalor, with no proper homes, without potable drinking water, no health care, anemic amenities, lack of educational opportunities, and scarcity of jobs and job skills that are necessary to allow them to earn a proper living. Their main source of employment is engaging in manual labor, working for others who pay them substandard wages. These impoverished people dot the entire world.

The question that arises from this condition is, "Can this be considered fair and equitable?" A fair-minded person would come to the logical conclusion that something is definitely wrong with this situation. One can correctly describe this situation as simply unjust, with no real *balance* as it relates to this segment of the population. Is this coincidence or just happenstance? This phenomenon lends itself to what can be called an *imbalance* in societal treatment and perpetual resentment. It eventually leads to uprisings and chaos in the populace.

It is the responsibility of all who are in charge of people to demonstrate the *balanced* leadership skills required to ensure that all people live in dignity. People should not be deprived of the basic necessities of daily living. They and their children should not go to bed suffering from the want of shelter and food.

In this part of the developed world, most workers fall into two categories: unionized and non-unionized.

The many benefits given to the non-unionized employees are dependent on their performance and that of the company. Their pay increases (including benefits like health care and vacation time) are generally determined by leadership and given to them on an annual basis.

To determine who will get an increase in salary, many companies have a ranking system for employees, ranging from 1 for excellent to 5 for poor (designated for possible termination of employment). Generally, on the scale, about 10 percent of employees are ranked a 1, and about 10 percent are ranked a 5. The rest of the employees (80 percent) receive a ranking of 2 to 4. Most of these employees are ranked 3. Based on this formula, most of the employees get a pay raise reflecting of cost of living. Some lucky employees receive bonuses and promotions based on the company's performance and maybe on their need.

At the time of pay increases (usually yearly), many employees who are ranked 2, 3, or 4 are very disgruntled because their individual rankings decide their pay increases. The ranking system just described is generally skewed, and most high-performing employees are not satisfied with their ranking or their pay increases. Most employees find this system unequitable and unbalanced, often subjective, and fraught with favoritism.

Unionized workers' pay increases are dependent on the success of their negotiators. These employees have the option of not signing the company's offer, and they can elect to go on strike, based on the many conditions outlined in their contract. Some strikes are resolved quickly. On occasion, strikes can go on for a relatively long duration (basically shutting down the company).

All unionized workers generally receive a negotiated wage increase. Their increase is not based on the kind of ranking system outlined above for non-unionized workers. Generally, one can say that because of the conditions negotiated and approved in their contract, these employees consider themselves to be treated more equitably and in a more *balanced* manner.

There are also many other examples of the use of the word *balance*. For example, it can be used to describe a person's emotional state, an opinion, the regulation of a clock or watch, an account balance, an apparatus for weighing, such as two scales with a central pivot, balancing work and family life, the scales of justice, and a meaning in the religious context, to measure one's good and bad deeds.

> *"Balance, peace, and joy are the fruit of a successful life. It starts with recognizing your talents and finding ways to serve others by using them."*
>
> **– Thomas Kinkade**

Balance is written by Mohamid Mobin

"Don't tell me what you believe in. I'll observe how you behave and I will make my own determination."

– Alex Trebek

Behave

be·have

/bəˈhāv/

Verb

1. *Act or conduct oneself in a specified way, especially toward others*

2. *Conduct oneself in accordance with the accepted norms of a society or group*

Mike Myers's character, Austin Powers, is famous for saying the one line, "Oh...*behave*"... in that drawn-out British accent. He was saying, "Do not be naughty."

I overheard a mother declare to her three children in my office the other day, "Now, you kids need to behave in here today, or I won't get you smoothies later." At that moment, I wondered exactly what she really meant by that. There must have been a preset standard she was expecting them to not only know, but follow.

If you have ever been in trouble, you would want to learn how to behave. Especially if it was a recurring issue and had costly consequences. So how do we, as adults, learn to behave? The progression of the word itself is unique. "Behave" is made of two words: "be" and "have." So apparently, when you behave correctly, you can *be* something and *have* something. The first word is "be," so in order to have, you must first be. In other words, it's more than just a simple behavior. *I believe it is a being that produces having, which then impacts behavior.*

Perhaps we think the easier way to our goal is just the action itself. Therapists call this "behavior modification," a term that refers to behavioral-change procedures that were employed during the 1970s and early 1980s. Based on methodological behaviorism, overt behavior was modified with presumed consequences, including artificial positive and negative reinforcement contingencies to increase desirable behavior. Or it involves administering positive and negative punishment and/or extinction to reduce problematic behavior.

The problem is, if all we do is change what we do (just to get what we want), did we really change? Are we really being or just pretending? Behavior can be changed or modified with the slightest of effort, thus allowing even the smallest circumstances to alter our desired results. *But*, if our intent embodies the change and truly we live congruent to the expected behavior, then we are being.

If you think of the word and focus on the *be* part first, like mentioned, the *have* part will follow. After all, we are human *beings*, not simply human *doings*.

The question is, then, how do we...*be*? I guess we first need to figure out what we want to have. Like Steven Covey declares in his famous work, *The 7 Habits of Highly Successful People*, "begin with the end in mind."

I believe that to *be* is actually to *become*. It is not an accident. It is an intentional, well-planned outcome. A desired path of accomplishment, beginning with your ultimate goal in mind.

So the questions for each of us are, what do we want? What do we want to be? What do we want to become? Thus, how do we want to behave?

To help answer these questions for yourself, follow these four B's, or Be's, of behavior:

1. **Be humble.** Learn from others. If you think you've got it all figured out, you're probably headed for a serious crash. Acknowledge that you are in need of change, and do not defend the wrong actions or conduct.

2. **Be surrounded by what you want.** It has been proven that our environment influences us. Our conduct is somewhat formed by what is positively or negatively reinforced by those around us.

3. **Be intentional.** When you are deliberately acting a certain way, you can be anything you choose to be. This develops your character, which eventually births your preconceived results. (Remember who you are trying to be!)

4. **Be considerate.** When you are sensitive to those around you, there will be clues if you are off course—you will notice the small signs. If your behavior is inconsiderate or inconsistent with the values you are trying to live by, then you should immediately say, "Please excuse me" or "I'm sorry!" If you mess up, get up, reposition yourself, and try again.

"We change our behavior when the pain of staying the same becomes greater than the pain of changing."

– Henry Cloud

Behave is written by Dr. Paul C. Sorchy II

"Be at war with your vices, at peace with your neighbors, and let every New Year find you a better man."

– Benjamin Franklin

Better

bet·ter

/ˈbedər/

Adjective

1. *Of a more excellent or effective type or quality*

2. *Partly or fully recovered from illness, injury, or mental stress; less unwell*

Adverb

1. *More excellently or effective*

Noun

1. *The better one; that which is better*

My innate desire since being a small child is to be *better*. A better baseball player, a better student, a better friend, a better son—being better than what my parents, teachers, and anyone in authority ever expected.

Those attempts to be better worked most of the time and resulted in good repercussions when I was young. Even when, during the fifth grade, I made up my mind that I would become the Paumanok Elementary School class president in the sixth grade. And what do you know, by beating Mary Marinaro, it happened! (Not really sure if I won because I was promising my classmates that Coke would flow from the water fountains if they voted for me).

My desire to be better came to a screeching halt in my adolescent years, when I realized my nature was not to become better, but rather, it was to be worse. There was a wisp of pleasure that would sweep over me when I became worse. It was fleeting but so made sense at that point because being better was too hard, and often my attempts would fall way short.

"Give it up," I thought, and I would stop trying to be better. What's the use? Having no pleasure and failing at being better led me to choose the selfish, gratifying effects of being worse. I chose the latter and lived that way for many years of teenagehood.

The "worse" living did have results associated with it. Those included hurting others, rebellion, police rides home, and generally living a C grade of life. I did not see in my future ever having a desire to be better again.

Until…I met my new friend, John, at the age of twenty. He was a go-getter with an amazing work ethic and leadership abilities. People loved being around him. He brought my better game back as he spoke into my life by exemplifying the many benefits of being better. The effort to become better did not seem like climbing Mt. Everest when John modeled it to me. It was like hitting singles in baseball—it didn't require too much effort, but I was strategic in where I placed my "hits."

Most of my hits occurred by changing my "teammates," the people in my life. I weeded the worse players out of my life and replaced them with those who were better. I started to hang with a "better" team. Those who had a better vision, a better attitude, a better sense of family, a better desire to succeed at work, etc.

An old adage says, "Iron sharpens iron." Surrounding myself with a new shortstop and coach who became welders to my rusty old worse lifestyle began my new life of becoming better. These teammates said little about being better but lived out a better lifestyle.

Don't try to hit home runs in becoming better; just aim for well-placed singles. Let other people who have a high, a better, batting average teach you how to become better. The runs will start to mount up with every better decision you make, until you look back and realize worse living was not your true calling.

Here are the ingredients you need in your life to become *better*:

B – Be patient; moving from worse to better will take time.

E – Every better decision gets you closer to an anti-worse lifestyle.

T – Trade out worse teammates for better ones.

T – Tell others about your single runs.

E – Each day brings new chances to become better.

R – Realize that a better story can be written about your life.

"Equip, encourage, and engage yourself to become better."

Better is written by Brian Buckley

"A brand for a company is like a reputation for a person. You earn reputation by trying to do hard things well."

– Jeff Bezos

/brand/

Noun

1. *A type of product manufactured by a particular company under a particular name*

2. *An identifying mark burned on livestock or (especially formerly) criminals or slaves with a branding iron*

Verb

1. *Mark with a branding iron*

2. *Assign a brand name to*

Branding has been my world for more than thirty years. I spent twenty years at Darden Restaurants, mostly at Red Lobster, where we spent more than $100 million per year on branding. We spent a total of more than $1 billion while I was there.

As part of that expense, we got to hire some of the most brilliant branding people in the world. My favorite influencer/mentor became Stan Richards, founder of the Richards Group. He who was responsible for the Cow Campaign for Chick-fil-A, as well as branding for Home Depot, Motel 6, and many other companies. I learned many branding secrets from him.

In 2008, I set out on my own and decided to start Brand Catalyst Partners, a brand consultancy firm committed to helping CEOs and their teams align with their highest compelling truths. With the support of Stan Richards and a well-developed branding process, I've now helped more than one hundred organizations. My vision is "inspiring brands to live their highest promise." That guides every decision I make.

The word "brand" is rich with many meanings. And, while it is usually associated with a product or service, it also applies to individuals. Let's explore how it applies to you and me.

What's in a name? Mother Teresa, Nelson Mandela, Oprah Winfrey, Winston Churchill, Gandhi, Walter Cronkite. Each name brings about certain thoughts and impressions in our minds, right?

A few more: Matt Lauer, Lori Laughlin, Bill Hybels, Kevin Spacey, Lance Armstrong, O. J. Simpson. Yikes! Hmmm…at one time, these people and their names were known for their talent and influence. Now it's a much different story. Our paradigms about these people have been forever changed because of their poor decisions. A simple mention of their names brings up immediate thoughts. Reputations are fragile.

Warren Buffet said, "It takes twenty years to build a reputation and only five minutes to lose it." How true is that!

What comes to people's minds when they think of *you*? Maybe you know; maybe you don't. But either way, from this point on, be intentional about who you want to be and how you want to be known.

When interviewing people, I love to ask the question, "Who are you?" Most people's first response is, "My name is...." Then, most struggle to find the right words to describe who they are. Of course they can rattle off their basic roles in life like father, mother, husband, wife, etc. But beyond basic labels, many struggle. Then many even say, "No one has ever asked me that question before."

If you struggle at all to express "who you are," give yourself three minutes to answer the questions below:

1. Whose hero were you created to be?

2. What promise did God make the world when He made you?

You can't be everything to everyone. But you can be something to someone. The answer to these questions will help you find meaning.

Here is another set of "fog-cutting questions" along the same lines:

1. Who do you want to help?

2. How do you want to help them?

Answering these questions will help you focus all decision making in your life. Each daily decision you make will help you build the reputation that supports your true identity, not some manufactured identity that you struggle to maintain because others think you should.

This exercise is more important now than ever. Why? Because social media has created a whole new world of false identity and comparison the world has never seen before. Does it really matter what all your Facebook friends think about you? Are they coming to your funeral? Do they really matter? If you find yourself posting things to intentionally support an identity what may not be true, why are you doing it? Sooner or later, you'll have an identity crisis.

Conversely, if you can use social media to help reach people you want to help, go for it! Social media can be a great amplifier of your identity and your message. The new world is full of people who created a personal brand using social media. The opportunity has never been greater. Ever heard of

Michael Hyatt (www.michaelhyatt.com)? He used the internet and social media to build a thriving empire to help authors and business leaders!

I'll leave you with this personal story…

In the late summer of 1980, I can distinctly remember getting in my car to leave for college. As I sat in the driver's seat, looking out the open window at my father, he was at a loss for words and started getting a little emotional. He realized my days of childhood were coming to an end. He was looking for some parting words. He finally said, "Remember, you are a Burch." It's as if he was summarizing almost twenty years of training and upbringing in one word—our last name, Burch.

He was summarizing everything he taught me by mentioning that one thing, our last name. What does *your* last name mean? Better yet, what does your *full* name mean?

If you have never written your own obituary, maybe now is the time. These two questions should help you:

1. Who do you want to speak on your behalf at your funeral?

2. What would you like them to say?

3. What would you like them *not* to say?

> *"A good name is more desirable than great riches; to be esteemed is better than silver or gold."*
>
> **– King Solomon**

Brand is written by Kennan Burch

"Champions are not the ones who always win races—champions are the ones who get out there and try. And try harder the next time. And even harder the next time. 'Champion' is a state of mind. They are devoted. They compete to best themselves as much, if not more than, they compete to best others. Champions are not just athletes."

—**Simon Sinek**

Champion

cham·pi·on

/ˈCHampēən/

Noun

1. *A person who has defeated or surpassed all rivals in a competition, especially in sports*

2. *A person who fights or argues for a cause or on behalf of someone else*

Verb

1. *Support the cause of; defend*

Let's face it, when we think of *champions*, we think about people who *win*.

I sure want to win in life. Don't you? You wouldn't be reading this if you didn't.

If we look at the lives of champions up close, as if through a magnifying glass, we see a theme of consistency. They show up to competitions, presentations, conversations, whatever…with a predictable attitude and level of focus. Their actions are aligned with who they are.

It's amazing.

Just how can they be that consistent day in and day out, despite all the odds…despite the many people trying to knock them off course? That's the million-dollar question when watching the world's greatest athletes, entrepreneurs, and executives.

You see, most people jump right into the game of life focused on *how* to win. "*How* can I get this raise? *How* can I win this competition? *How* can I impress this person? *How* can I win this deal? *How* can I build this business?"

Don't get me wrong, asking the *how* question is the right thing to do. It just needs two companions to go before it: *what* and *who*.

Without these, the game of life is filled with being overwhelmed, exhausted, and irritable. I know this from firsthand experience.

For three years, I was winning as an entrepreneur in sports and business. I was climbing that mountain of success. I knew *how* to get the job done, and I did it well. To the world, I was reaching *champion* status.

But I wasn't really winning. I had lost my oxygen. I was sleeping poorly because my brain was in overdrive. I was constantly stressed because I was never satisfied with my work. And I was losing my family and closest relationships because of it.

I was so focused on *how* I could become a champion in sports and business that I forgot about the purpose of my work and who it actually impacted. I never had a clear *what* and *who*. I didn't know what I was fighting for.

I lost sight of *who* I was fighting for.

True *champions* are crystal clear about their *what* and *who* before they identify the *how*. And with clarity comes consistency.

Think about driving a car on a highway. When you're clear about the speed limit, you know at what speed you should keep your car moving. If no speed limit were posted, you would be wondering, "How fast should I go?"

Our speed limit in life is our *what* and *how*.

When we're clear about *what* we're fighting for in this season of life, it becomes easier to say no to the distractions...to make one decision over another. When we're clear about *who* we're fighting for, it becomes easier to get up on the days when our minds and bodies tell us to stay put. It gives us the extra drive to push past the hurdles that get in our way.

If you want to be a champion, you must seek clarity about your *what* and *who* before the *how*.

Ask yourself these first two questions below to get clarity on your *what* and *who*. The last two questions will help you identify the *how*. Notice they all start with "W"...the first letter of the word *win*:

1. What do you want in this season of your life?

2. Who's counting on you?

3. What do you need to *start* doing to accomplish your *what* and come through for your *who*?

4. What do you need to *stop* doing to accomplish your *what* and come through for your *who*?

Letting the *what* and *who* come before the *how* requires a mindset shift. And the mind is where champions are made.

Did you catch that? *Champions* are made, not born.

Make that shift today because *champion* status is ultimately up to you—and *you* deserve it!

"I hated every minute of training, but I said, 'Don't quit. Suffer now and live the rest of your life as a champion.'"
—Muhammad Ali

Written by James Reid (J. R.)

"Start doing what's necessary, then do what's possible, and suddenly you are doing the impossible."

—St. Francis of Assisi

Coach (1)
Noun

1. A horse-drawn carriage, especially a closed one

2. A railroad car

Verb

1. Travel by coach.

Adverb

1. In economy class, accommodations in an aircraft or train

Coach (2)
Noun

1. An athletic instructor or trainer

Verb

1. Train or instruct (a team or player)

Origin of "Coach"

It was so interesting to me when I discovered where the word *coach* derived from originally.

It all started way back in the fifteenth century in a small town named Kocs, on the main road between Vienna and Budapest, Austria. As the story goes, a transportation company created a carriage with more space and more comfort. It was called a *kocsi*, short for *kocsi szeker* or "cart of Kocs." The concept of the *kocsi* eventually became popular throughout Europe. In Germany, it was a *kutsche*; in France, it was called a *coche*, and in England, it was a *coach*.

"Coach" as a Metaphor

As time progressed, the meaning has been adapted, and the everyday use of "coach" is a metaphor.

First applied in education, the word "coach" in eighteenth-century England was a verb that referred to tutors helping students prepare for exams. The tutors enabled the students to quickly and comfortably achieve their goal of passing their exams and progressing to the next stage of their education.

When I was a young boy growing up in Arkansas, my father was a pastor, so even though we had a house with four boys, none of us played sports. Thus, we were not introduced to a sports coach, as such. We were all busy helping with the demands of a small congregation. I suspect I could have played for the NFL as a defensive lineman because when I got married, I was a solid 159 pounds of pure muscle. Fortunately, that dream was shattered!

Since then, I have worked with hundreds of collegiate athletes and their coaches for many years. I have seen many cases in which a coach changed a boy's life! But I still did not connect the dots until recently. You see, for me, the idea of a sports coach yelling and barking out instructions and corrections is what comes to mind when I think about coaching. That is far from the mental image of a comfortable carriage ride that is taking someone from where they are to where they want to go.

Story of a Memorable Coach

Recently I saw a viral video of a high school football coach who realized that he had an opportunity to not just coach football but to help take student athletes on the journey to become young men, both on and off the field.

As the season came to a close with a record of 8–4, the team had made it to the playoffs but was losing in the first round, Coach Cody Gross of Athens, Alabama, decided to start what he called "Manly Mondays." The concept was to give the male student athletes tools to help them navigate life. "We taught them how to look a man in the eye and give a good, firm handshake," Gross said. "And they couldn't leave the locker room until they did that."

The coach also taught the young men how to change a flat tire, as well as how to change the oil in a car. "The big thing is, as coaches, we can have a big impact on young men," he continued. "That's why I do what I do. When (last) season ended, I felt the need to be more intentional about some of the things we do. We try to model the behaviors we expect."

"We are trying to teach them life lessons," he added. "It's not just about coaching football. Any sport teaches you about life, but I don't think any sport teaches you the hard knocks of life more than football. You get knocked down. You get back up. It's a great lesson, but there is more to it than the winning and losing and coaching a kid how to play football."

Business Coaching

As a business coach, I now define *coaching* as facilitating intentional conversations that help the person I am engaged with develop a mindset that allows him or her to experience the transformation needed to achieve destiny.

Many times, my coaching sessions go beyond just working with clients on how to create the right systems and business plans. Often, we talk about many areas of life outside their businesses, from relationships with their spouses to how they are working to lead their children. As we try to help leaders become the best they can be, we discover that if they are challenged in leading relationships at work, they have similar challenges away from the workplace.

Practically speaking, here are three ways I provide value as a coach:

1. I use powerful questions to spur discovery and facilitate growth.

2. I help clients map out the actions that lead to change.

3. I focus on the aspirations and agenda of each client.

> *"Everyone needs a coach. It doesn't matter whether you're a basketball player, a tennis player, a gymnast, or a bridge player."*
>
> **—Bill Gates**

Coach is written by Nobel Bowman

"Competence is a great creator of confidence."

—Mary Jo Putney

Competence

com·pe·tence

/ˈkämpədəns/

Noun

1. *The ability to do something successfully or efficiently*

2. *(Dated) An income large enough to live on, typically unearned*

Do you have "what it takes?" It's a common phrase. Having *what it takes* to succeed in life is something we all strive for. Being competent—having *competence*—means we have what it takes. We have not just the skills, but the drive, the judgment, and the opportunity to achieve our dreams.

So how do we become competent? I've devoted my life to helping young people, our nation's youth, gain the competence they need to live with confidence.

As parents and marketplace leaders, we look to our education system to enable our kids to be competent. Sadly, in far too many sectors of this country, we are failing at that objective. If our schools were given a report card, far too many would not receive a passing grade. Why is that? Is it the curriculum? Is it the environment? The teachers? The funding?

There are no easy answers, but it starts with recognizing that to be competent requires more than just knowing the right answer to a problem. Consider your current favorite song. You can sing the melody line in time with the words to the song. However, if that's all you heard in your head, I suspect it wouldn't be your favorite song for very long. Why? Because what you hear in your head is a beautiful assembly of instruments, artfully arranged. You hear the rhythms, horns, keyboards, guitar licks, and harmonies, all working together to create the magic that you hear with your ears and that stirs your soul.

So it is with creating competent kids. Yes, they need certain basic knowledge. But having the right information is not enough. That knowledge needs to be paired with the motivation to use it and with the wisdom and judgment to apply it properly. That knowledge needs to be given the right opportunity.

As a leader, how can you inspire competence? Look around you. Consider where you can promote these components of competence:

1. **Knowledge**. What do you know that needs to be shared with others? How can your training and experience be passed on?

2. **Motivation**. How can your words and actions inspire people to rise, to dream to achieve, to be the best version of themselves possible?

3. **Judgment**. People make choices every day, not all of them good. How can you impart wisdom that will help those around you make better judgment calls?

4. **Skill**. Experience breeds skill. The more you do something, the better at it you get. Practice makes perfect. Where can your experience be used to enhance competence?

5. **Strength**. Sometimes it takes real willpower, persistence, determination, and fortitude to press through. You know the old saying, "When the going gets tough, the tough get going." How can you inspire strength in others?

6. **Opportunity**. To become competent requires some level of opportunity. What doors can you open for others? How can you create opportunity for someone else to become more competent?

As a nation, we are always one generation away from greatness or failure. Let's rededicate ourselves to creating competence, especially in our young people.

"One of the best uses of your time is to increase your competence in your key result areas."

—Brian Tracy

Competence is written by Dr. Clarence Nixon

"You control your future, your destiny. What you think about comes about. By recording your dreams and goals on paper, you set in motion the process of becoming the person you most want to be. Put your future in good hands—your own."

—Mark Victor Hansen

Control

con·trol

[kənˈtrōl]

Noun

1. *The power to influence or direct people's behavior or the course of events*

2. *A group or individuals used as a standard of comparison for checking the results of a survey or experiment*

Verb

1. *Determine the behavior or supervise the running of*

2. *Take into account (an extraneous factor that might affect results) when performing an experiment*

The word *control* gets a bad rap!

Perhaps it is mostly because of problematic ideas like being a "control freak" or the need to manipulate all outcomes. True, control can be a very ugly quality when embodied in unhealthy ways, and it can be somewhat silly under very normal circumstances.

We sports fans are notorious for blaming coaches, players, and even officials when our team goes down in defeat. It may be annoying to hear your workmate go on and on about play calling and the gamut of home-field advantages, but it's also annoying when the kicker, in American football, misses an easy field goal well within his range. We may not take time to think about wind conditions, delivery of the ball, placement by the holder, and a few very large, strong, angry players charging hard at the (usually) very small ex-soccer player. Yet a game or a match lost has ruined many a weekend for grown-ups across this globe.

And it is completely out of our control. I can understand how the kicker may feel the pain, but it almost makes no sense at all for me to lose a moment over it. So, for this quick take on a really big idea, let's focus on spinning control in a positive way. Think about this.

We get "mind drift," whether it is related to a past experience or an upcoming challenge. Perhaps we project out to next Wednesday, mentally playing out an important sales presentation, planning and imagining outcomes. There is certainly a need for this kind of thinking. Here's the angle I'd like to take, couched in a few questions:

1. Can the physical human body live in the past or in the future? No.

2. Where can it exist? In the present moment.

3. Can the human mind live in the past or in the future? Yes.

4. Where does it struggle to exist? In the present moment.

Lou Holtz is the legendary college football coach who made his name as head coach of the Fighting Irish of Notre Dame, with a number of successful seasons topped by a National Championship. He passionately preaches the acronym WIN, which stands for "What's Important Now?" To align our minds and bodies in the present can be challenging, but if we really want to WIN, we must wrestle with this question. After all, it's the only thing we can possibly control. What's done is done, and what will be is to be determined partly by what we choose to do in this moment.

What happens now is likely impacted by our course of action or a decision we make. The "right now" moment may also be directed by initiating a conversation or literally putting pen to paper right here and right now, while the idea is white-hot. Otherwise, the moment is gone forever.

A verse in Ecclesiastes says, "There is a time for everything under the sun." True. But what's important now? If preparation for the presentation is what's important *now*, then by all means, let's be diligent. If listening to my workmate share her concerns for my plan and then hearing her out is what's important now, then that's what I will do in this moment.

This moment, right now, is when we have the highest potential for impact.

Dr. Amber Selking, in her excellent podcast "Building Championship Mindsets," says, "Attentional control is about placing our attention on the right things at the right time." She goes on to explain that there are two basic modes of distraction: internal and external. In other words, when the 15-mph crosswind is blowing and the rain has begun to fall, our friend the placekicker had better be managing the conditions rather than his internal fear of shanking the attempt.

We often struggle to distinguish what we *want* to control from what we *need* to control and what we simply *can't* control. It is within reason to say that this will continue to be a struggle at some level. But when we wrestle with the WIN question, we have the chance to get a fresh perspective on ways to affect outcomes with clarity and purpose.

Here are three steps to help you accomplish that:

1. Pay attention to where your thoughts go.

2. Place your attention on the right things at the right time.

3. Practice identifying what can and should be controlled.

> *"Attentional control is about placing our attention on the right things at the right time."*
>
> **—Dr. Amber Selking**

Control is written by Edgar Cabello

"All our dreams can come true, if we have the courage to pursue them."

—Walt Disney

/ˈkərij/

Noun

1. *The ability to do something that frightens one*

One of my favorite stories to share is one about Walt Disney's vision for creating Disneyland.

Born out of a desire to spend more time with his children and have more control over the entertainment he was creating, his idea was met with resistance. Both Walt's wife, Lillian, and his own brother, Roy, didn't think the amusement industry was one Walt should consider, given the public perception of carnivals and traveling fairs.

Walt's persistence was grounded in his family values. Every Saturday, he would take his daughters to local parks for a little fun. Unfortunately, there wasn't much for Walt to do there because everything was sized for children, not adults. It was in this situation that Walt later said, "I just thought there should be a place where parents and their children could have fun together."

It was in that same decade that Walt attempted to bring a multisensory experience to audiences through the release of *Fantasia* in 1940. Unfortunately, due to the costs associated with bringing this type of experience to theaters and the unwillingness of theater owners to take the financial risks in doing so, the film did not perform well. Walt knew that if he was to take his studio to new heights, he was going to have to have more control over his product.

Walt saw an opportunity to merge his values and his vision together in an ambitious endeavor called Disneyland. With local opposition, skeptical friends and family, loans from multiple banks, and everything he owned on the line, Disneyland opened in 1955 at a cost of $17 million. Although not everything was perfect on opening day, one thing surpassed everyone's expectations: the number of people who showed up.

Having anticipated fifteen thousand guests, more than twenty-eight thousand visited the park on opening day. Even with all the opening-week struggles, more than one million guests visited Disneyland. Walt's *courage* ultimately paid off.

Often, when we think of *courage*, we think about the heroic moments or stories we have seen on the big screen, read in a good book, or observed in someone else. Rarely do we consider our own stories or moments to be examples of courage. Whether we live in uncertainty about how we might respond had we been in similar situations or diminish the value of our own simple moments of courage, we must consider the core motivation for courage.

The etymology of the word "courage" begins with the Latin word *cor*, which means "heart." In other words, long before we used the word "courage," we used the word *cor*, challenging ourselves to "have heart." It is from the heart that we find courage. Courage is born in the heart. We now know what the ancients knew long ago: that courage comes from the heart.

From the heart, we move to the mind. The modern definition of "courage" emphasizes both "mental and moral strength," helping us define two things at the core of our being:

1. What we value

2. What we want to achieve in life

We now realize that at the core of courage is the heart to believe in something we want to achieve and what we value most. What we want to achieve and what we value are often determined by how far we are willing to go to pursue something and what we are willing to do to protect it.

I challenge you, over the course of this week, to compose two lists:

1. A list of the things you value most in life

2. A list of the things you want to achieve in life

Once the lists are complete, prioritize the things you want to achieve in life in one column, and then prioritize your values in the other column. Then associate every value you identified with the things you want to achieve in life by drawing lines from one column to the other. Once complete, you will have a personal value system established from the heart that will help drive you toward your goals in life with courage.

Now that you have created these lists, each day this week, read them out loud, one by one.

Next, look for opportunities throughout the day to make decisions based on your values and goals. At the end of the day, examine what you did to help you get closer to each.

"Success is not final, failure is not fatal: it is the courage to continue that counts."

—Winston Churchill

Courage is written by Jon Langford

"It's kind of fun to do the impossible."

—Walt Disney

Creative

cre·a·tive

/krēˈādiv/

Adjective

1. *Relating to or involving the imagination or original ideas, especially in the production of an artistic work*

Noun (Informal)

1. *A person who is creative, typically in a professional context*

Think back to when you were young. What was your favorite day of the year? You are probably imagining your birthday, right? That special day once a year when you got extra attention, plenty of cake and ice cream, and of course, every kid's favorite: *presents*!

What child doesn't love presents? But as you may recall, there's something funny about children and gifts. No matter if it was a brand-new bike or the latest, greatest toy, most of us eventually found ourselves putting down the gift itself in favor of playing with the giant cardboard box it came in.

This box was our castle. Our spaceship. Our fort. And for good reason. During this time in our early childhood, we were all thinking "expansively." Our little minds knew no constraints, and so through the power of Divergent

Thinking, a simple box could be anything our hearts desired.

But then one day along came school. Soon enough, we had teachers telling us that our favorite spaceship is "just a box," and in that split second all of our creativity and imagination started to crumble. This would go on to be compounded by traditional education and employment, where we were taught to think "reductively" (Convergent Thinking) instead of Expansively. The endless leaps and bounds of our imaginations were reeled in and confined.

This is why so many people believe they are not *creative*. Instead of thinking *Expansively* and believing anything is possible, they were taught to think *Reductively* and to believe that "Creativity" was a special skill set limited to the ability to play music, paint, or act.

Personally, I have a much broader view of creativity. *We are all creative.* We all played with the box once upon a time and turned it into a vehicle that sailed the seas or reached the stars. But we have been told we're not creative so many times that we've simply given up, and now we leave creativity to the "creatives."

I define *creativity* as the ability to have an idea and *innovation* as the ability to get it done. But like every other muscle, your creative brain (the right side) needs regular exercise. Thankfully, I have five simple tips to exercise the creative part of your mind to improve creativity:

1. Go for a Walk

Both Walt Disney and Steve Jobs could always be found walking the campuses of Disney Studios, Pixar, and Apple. Indeed, they would tell you it was these walks where they got their best ideas. So, find time each day to get out from behind your desk and get some creative inspiration while out on a stroll!

2. Seek Freshness

Have you ever gotten home from your commute, only to wonder how you got there? Believe it or not, your brain shuts down on the way home because there is never any fresh stimulus. It's the same car, the same route, the same sights, and the same sounds.

I'm a great believer that "no new stimulus in" equals "no new ideas out." Try commuting a different way to work once a month, and see what you notice that wasn't there before. Listen to a different radio station once a week. Even small changes can have a profound effect on how your brain functions, and these new stimuli could be just the thing you need to kickstart creativity.

3. Be Curious

Einstein famously once said, "I am not particularly clever, I am just innately curious."

As kids, didn't we ask "why, why, and why" again? Asking "why" was how we learned. But then education and corporate training taught us there is only one right answer, so we stopped looking for the second one.

Creativity and the insight for innovation often come from asking the fourth or fifth "why," never just the first one. So, condition yourself to keep asking why, and you'll find new creative ideas become magically unlocked.

4. Practice Mindfulness

We all know our daily calendars look like the bar code on the side of a cereal box. We also know that time is generally considered to be the biggest barrier to innovation, yet we continue to pack our diaries with meeting after meeting and then complain, "I don't have time to think!"

Scheduling a mindfulness routine can counteract this endless cycle. Try meditating first thing in the morning. Even as little as five minutes can help, especially if you are one of those people who gets their best ideas while falling asleep or waking up.

5. Be Playful

Did you know that only 13 percent of your brain is conscious, and the other 87 percent is subconscious? We use only 13 percent on any given day because when we're stressed at work, the reticular activation system (think of it as a door inside your mind) between the conscious and subconscious brain is firmly closed.

Yet the moment we play and laugh, that door opens, giving us access to both sides of our brains. It's these moments when creative solutions to problems can really shine through. So take advantage, and work at times during the day when you can let your brain "play"!

With these quick, easy exercises, you'll be able to greatly enhance your ability to function creatively on a daily basis and reactivate that expansive thinking from your childhood. And with enough practice, not only will you be an unstoppable force of creativity and innovation; you'll find yourself turning every box you see back into a spaceship!

"We keep moving forward, opening new doors, and doing new things because we're curious, and curiosity keeps leading us down new paths."

—Walt Disney

Creative is written by Duncan Wardle

"Culture eats strategy for breakfast."

—Peter Drucker

Culture

cul·ture

/ˈkəlCHər/

Noun

1. The arts and other manifestations of human intellectual achievement regarded collectively

2. The customs, arts, social institutions, and achievements of a particular nation, people, or other social group

Verb

1. Maintain (tissue cells, bacteria, etc.) in conditions suitable for growth

There are lots of books out there to read on how to foster an inclusive *culture* that touches *everyone*, a culture that respects *everyone*, a culture that makes *everyone* feel special, a culture that treats *everyone* as an individual, and a culture that provides developmental opportunities for *everyone*, so that each and every individual can achieve the level of his or her own ability.

Here's how you can think about workplace culture: while *diversity* focuses on our differences and similarities, workplace *culture* focuses on the respect and appreciation we show one another, so no one feels left out. Feelings are a big deal. If people *feel* left out, then they *are* left out.

To put it even more simply, workplace culture is making sure that everyone matters…and that everyone *knows* that he or she matters.

We make people feel included by talking and listening to them, recognizing them, knowing them well, and developing them. At the least, we assist them with their development by encouraging them and by getting them into the right kind of training.

The problem is that it is not going to work as well unless *everyone* is doing this. This is a no-brainer because if people feel excluded, whether it is because someone is preoccupied and not paying attention or for some other reason, then the idea of inclusion is lost.

Creating the right culture is one of the main responsibilities of a leader. The great leaders do this especially well. Whether it is at home or at work, the culture matters, and we as leaders have control over that culture. To create a healthy, respectful, trustworthy culture at work, we all need to set the example by paying attention to everybody, by showing respect to everybody, and by being available for everybody who needs to see us. At a minimum, we must find another way to assist them if we are not available.

As everyone continues to learn about the importance of an inclusive culture and goes about practicing being inclusive, we will continue to have a special culture that is crisp, clean, and clear in every way and makes everybody want to stay and have their careers in our organizations.

We all know to some degree how it feels to be excluded. I remember that when I joined a couple of companies in my career, I was excluded because I was not an "insider."

On one occasion, I was somewhat excluded because of where I was from—Oklahoma—and because I had not received my formal training from the "right" hospitality school. I felt excluded in junior high school from the "in crowd" as well. That may have been my imagination, but that is still the way I felt. This is not a good feeling, and it can take its toll on one's self-esteem and self-confidence, which can be key factors in how someone's life turns out. I have finally recovered!

We need to take this very seriously. We need to pay attention to everyone. Responsibility is not self-serving. It is about the future: the future of the organization, the future of our families, and the future of the people we work with.

Great leaders build up people's self-esteem and self-confidence. If you have children, you know how important it is to focus on each child in a way that makes each one feel special, which may not be the way to make the others feel special. Think back to when you were a child and how important this was to you. You know it is vital to treat children as individuals and to show complete respect to them and to develop them. It is easy to do with your children because you know them very well, if you are paying attention.

It is the same way with your fellow team members. *If you know them well, then you will treat them well.* It is also a no-brainer that when people feel respected and valued for the talents and skills they bring to the team, they feel more motivated and inspired, which leads to commitment.

When people are committed, they feel a strong personal connection with the work they do. Every single role at the organization is important. If it is not important, we should not have that role. You will find that the more inclusive your work environment is, the more people will want to be a part of your team. Being known for being inclusive will help you recruit and retain the very best team members, which will help ensure that you get the right business results. Turnover in your group will be extremely low, as will disciplinary problems, sick-day usage, and on and on.

As a leader at home or work, it is your responsibility to create a culture in which everybody can thrive. Here are six tips for accomplishing that:

1. **Commit to learn more about how to create and manage a culture by reading about the subject.** Take seminars on culture to become an expert with a total understanding of your role in this endeavor. The Disney Institute is a great source for this learning.

2. **Commit to developing the why for this endeavor.** Communicate it to all of your team members.

3. **Commit to be the perfect role model for the culture you are striving to create.**

4. **Commit to total clarity about the importance of creating a culture in which everybody matters and they know they matter.**

5. **Commit to making the hard decision and having the hard conversations to achieve results.**

6. **Commit your learning and strategy to writing.** Develop a document everybody can understand and use to learn about the subject of culture and your expectations of their roles and support.

Remember, great leaders build up people's self-esteem and self-confidence.

"Our belief is that if you get the culture right, most of the other stuff, like great customer service or building a great long-term brand, or empowering passionate employees and customers will happen on its own."

—Tony Hsieh, CEO, Zappos

Culture is written by Lee Cockerell

"Discipline is the bridge between goals and accomplishment."

—Jim Rohn

Discipline

dis·ci·pline

/ˈdisəplən/

Noun

1. *The practice of training people to obey rules or a code of behavior, using punishment to correct disobedience*

2. *A branch of knowledge, typically one studied in higher education*

Verb

1. *Train (someone) to obey rules or a code of behavior, using punishment to correct disobedience*

If you are like most people, when you saw the word *discipline*, you thought seriously about skipping this chapter. It just isn't one of those words that excites the senses. It is, however, one of those words that, when embraced, separates the good from the great.

The truth is that discipline is required to achieve and maintain greatness. The problem for many of us is that we see discipline as drudgery. Your commitment to be your best encouraged you to read this book. And your commitment to discipline in key areas of your life could change your destiny.

Think of a great athlete like swimmer Michael Phelps, the winningest Olympian of all time. He has won twenty-eight medals, including a record eight gold medals at the 2008 Olympic Games. Phelps didn't wake up when he was fifteen and say, "I think I will qualify for the 2000 Olympics." He began swimming when he was seven, at the encouragement of his mom to have an outlet for his energy. His parents were told he would never be able to focus on anything. His coach since age eleven acknowledges that Phelps spent a great deal of time on the side of the pool for bad behavior. He was later diagnosed with Attention Deficit Disorder.

But discipline changed his life. According to Greg Johnston, founder of The Mentor + Project, from age fourteen through the Beijing Olympics, Phelps trained seven days a week, 365 days a year. He figured that by training also on Sundays, he got a fifty-two-training-day advantage on his competition. He spent six hours in the water each day. He was able to channel all his energy into one discipline that developed into one habit: swimming daily. It is staggering to consider that he alone has won more medals than 161 countries combined.

But let's face it—the thought of that level of commitment is overwhelming to most of us. We struggle to hold on to a New Year's resolution for two weeks, much less 365 days a year.

What if discipline were not so overwhelming? What if we didn't have to dread it or see it as something that takes a lifetime to acquire? What if a disciplined life were attainable within the confines of our daily routines?

Dr. Stan Beecham, a good friend of mine, is the author of *Elite Minds— Creating the Competitive Advantage and Elite Minds—How Winners Think Differently* (must-reads for those desiring to live their lives to the fullest). A few years ago, Stan sat down with me as I struggled to make a major career decision. As we talked through the pros and cons, he asked me why I was defending staying where I was when everything pointed toward my need to embrace the other opportunity. I offered many of the same reasons you likely have for staying as you are and not embracing all that life offers: not enough time, being comfortable where I was, people relying on me, etc. He listened, and then he shared the following story.

In the 1970s, there was a great deal of talk about television being detrimental to the development of children. One day, a discussion broke out about this topic in the weight room at the University of Georgia. Players were throwing out their ideas when their strength coach, Sam Mrvos, walked in. One of the players asked him how much TV he allowed his children to watch. He responded, "As much as they want."

They were surprised and wondered aloud if he was joking. He just laughed and clarified that they could watch as much TV as they wanted—as long as they did push-ups during each commercial break. Not sure whether he was serious or not, the players dropped the subject. Several weeks later, one of Coach Mrvos's boys was at the field house with him when one of the football players remembered the discussion. That player decided to challenge the young boy to a push-up competition. Several other players jumped in. Gradually, all the players dropped out and watched as the coach's boy continued to do push-ups.

Here is the point: we often think of discipline as something that takes a lifetime of 24/7 focus to develop. Here was a young kid who didn't do push-ups all day long; he simply did them during the commercials. Yet he outperformed some of the best-conditioned athletes of his day.

Last year, I challenged myself to prove what was possible through discipline. I started by doing a few push-ups during every TV commercial, with the goal of doing the equivalent of my age every day. I was fifty-four when I started and struggled to do ten push-ups at a time. But I continued and soon found fifty-four too easy. I decided to increase my daily goal to one hundred. Within a few weeks, I was no longer challenged by one hundred. I set a new goal of 50,000 for the year and ultimately increased that goal to 100,000. In 2017—through discipline—I did more than 110,000 push-ups, all during commercial breaks.

What about you? What are the things you would do if you applied discipline to your goals? What are the commercial breaks in your life that you can use to make those goals a reality? The truth is, we have no idea what would be possible if we would simply apply discipline to our dreams!

The following are six important steps to achieving discipline in your life. The first letters of the steps form the acronym PUSH-UP:

P – **Pronounce your goal.** Accountability is key to maintaining discipline, so tell others what you hope to achieve.

U – **Understand your purpose.** This is the *why* behind the disciplined effort.

S – **Stay true to your goal.** When you dare to be disciplined, you challenge the mediocrity in others.

H – **Handle setbacks.** Setbacks due to sickness or schedule can't be avoided. But don't let a single miss derail you.

U – **Update your progress.** Consistent measurement is a vital part of discipline and encourages performance.

P – **Persevere.** Stay the course. Remember that discipline differentiates the good from the great.

"We have no idea what would be possible if we simply applied discipline to our dreams."

Discipline is written by Scott Humphrey

"There is a time when we must firmly choose the course which we will follow, or the endless drift of events will make the decision for us."

—Herbert V. Prochnow

/drift/

Verb

1. *Be carried slowly by a current of air or water*

2. *(Especially of snow or leaves) Be blown into heaps by the wind*

Noun

1. *A continuous slow movement from one place to another*

2. *The general intention or meaning of an argument or someone's remarks*

My idea of the word *drift* is a continuous slow movement that deviates from a set course of progress.

Drift reminds me of my New England winters as a child, looking out the window at the snowdrifts the morning after an overnight blizzard. As an adult now living by the ocean in Florida, *drift* reminds me of picking up *driftwood* on the beach that washed ashore the morning after an overnight of rough seas.

Closer to my heart is my concern for the residents in our program at Teen Challenge New England & New Jersey, who were under the power of addiction to drugs and alcohol. I do not want them to *drift* away from their sobriety. For them to *drift* just 1 degree off course could mean their death.

Drift happens slowly, unknowingly. Over time, you find yourself very far away from where you thought you were headed. It could be a gradual shift in your attitude or an inappropriate action that could eventually cost you your marriage, your job, or your life.

We are all prone to *drift* into "just this one" little white lie, taking what doesn't belong to us, "just peeking" at porn, holding a grudge, or having a one-night stand. But here is the true consequence of drifting away from our own personal core values:

- **D**rift
- **R**eally
- **I**ncreases
- **F**uture
- **T**rouble

No one and nothing is exempt from *drifting*. Entire corporations, organizations, businesses, and even churches and ministries can lose sight of their intended goals. Because we all have the propensity to *drift*, we must be very intentional about staying the course if we want to meet with success.

You're fortunate when you stay on course, walking steadily on the road revealed by God. You're blessed when you follow His directions. That's right—you don't go off on your own; you walk straight along the road He has set.

> *"Oh, that my steps might be steady, keeping to the course you set; Then I'll never have any regrets in comparing my life with your counsel."*
>
> **—David the Psalmist in Psalm 119:5–6 (MSG)**

On November 28, 1979, two hundred fifty-seven people were on board a large passenger jet, Air New Zealand flight TE901, for a sightseeing flight to Antarctica. Unknown to the pilots, someone had modified the flight coordinates by a mere two degrees. This small error caused the aircraft to *drift* twenty-eight miles to the east from where the pilots assumed they would be.

As they approached Antarctica, the pilots descended to a lower altitude to give the passengers a better view of the landscape. Although both were experienced pilots, neither had made this particular flight before, and they had no way of knowing that the incorrect coordinates had caused them to *drift* off course!

They were directly in the path of Mount Erebus, an active volcano that rises from the frozen landscape to a height of more than twelve thousand feet. As the pilots flew, the white of the snow and the ice covering the volcano blended with the white of the clouds above, making it appear as though they were flying over flat ground. They crashed into the side of the volcano, killing everyone on board. It was a terrible tragedy brought on by a minor error that caused the plane to *drift* off course by just two degrees.

As I look at the five letters of the word *drift*, I see that the "i" is dead center in the middle, while "d" and "r" are on the left side, and "f" and "t" are on the right. The "i" is balanced, sheltered, stable, safe, and protected. That "i" is you and me, and contrary to the word's definition, we can remain on course, never to be adrift or concerned about losing focus of our vision and goals.

"It's better to hang out with people better than you. Pick out associates whose behavior is better than yours, and you'll drift in that direction."

—Warren Buffett

Drift is written by Pasco Manzo

"Perhaps we are asking the wrong questions."

—The Matrix, 1999

Drive

drive

/drīv/

Verb

1. *Operate and control the direction and speed of a motor vehicle*

2. *Propel or carry along by force in a specified direction*

Noun

1. *A trip or journey in a car*

2. *(Psychology) An innate, biologically determined urge to attain a goal or satisfy a need*

What drives you? It is an important question. In my opinion, *drive* is the most important element of an exceptional life.

Yet so often, I see success teachers telling people to get a vision or a dream for their future. In truth, I have taught that concept many times myself! But a few years ago, I began to think that "What is your dream?" might be the wrong question. I now want to know, "What drives you?" I call that your *drive pedal*.

As my friend Harvey Mackay said, "I don't know of any entrepreneurs who have achieved any level of success without persistence and determination." Finding something that drives us is the prerequisite for great achievements…there can be no success without the drive to achieve it. Period.

There is no such thing as accidental, easy, lucky, or overnight success. Success is one of the most you've-got-to-want-it, didn't-see-that-coming, gotta-know-why pursuits in our lives. Before you take the on ramp to your road to success, tell yourself these four things:

1. I will have to make my own opportunities, and there will be times I don't see any.

2. It will be hard…probably harder than I think.

3. I will have to make my own luck and endure some bad luck.

4. It will take time, and I will have to be very patient.

In other words—and this is non-negotiable—it will take drive. Now, maybe you are a little depressed knowing how much work lies ahead for you. So go ahead and tell yourself one more thing:

It will be worth it!

At this point, I have identified how success does not happen…it does not happen easily. Now let's look at *drive* because as I said at the beginning, it is the one quality common to all achievers. In short, some might say that having a dream is the key to making your dreams come true…I would not.

A dream ≠ drive.

I know many great people who have dreamed artfully and focused on their dreams passionately, yet their dreams remain unfulfilled. Why is that? Because dreams birthed from a few hours of creative thinking and typed into the notes of your cell phone will not be:

- Courageous enough to attempt the impossible

- Ferocious enough to knock down barriers in your path

- Determined enough to endure the hardest of hardships along the way

- Resilient enough to hang on like grim death until the last millimeter of your nail breaks off!

That takes drive! That requires something primal within you, deeply rooted and unrelenting. It cannot be written on a legal pad…it's written in your soul. In fact, it must be a little angry, maybe even a little crazy.

Drive is born from years of processing experiences, some positive and many negative, that create very strong feelings about yourself and your future. Often, those experiences and the resulting feelings lead to a dream. But I am convinced that finding your drive is the most important first step, without which no other step matters.

Now, before the "dreamers" break out the pitchforks for me, let me offer my definition of drive:

Drive is a passion in your gut, forged in the fires of your past and present, that inspires a clear vision of your future, which you decide to relentlessly pursue right now.

There is an element of *dream* in drive…but drive is bigger, deeper, and in my opinion, more powerful.

Leadership trainer Israelmore Ayivor said it best: "Passion or drive is what moves the vehicle of a fulfilled life." The truth is, we do not have a *dream* problem; we have a *drive* problem. I know many leaders with a dream who are wondering what they did wrong (or what is wrong with them) that their dreams have not come true.

Do not be discouraged…you simply have run into this reality: you cannot count on a dream to fulfill a dream. And I believe those who point to their dream as a reason for their success do not realize it was actually their *drive* that got them there.

Now it's time to look within yourself and formulate what I call your *drive pedal*: that spectrum of experiences, relationships, and deep longings that creates an unstoppable passion to pursue your dream. Look in three areas:

Where do you hurt? Who do love? What do you want out of life?

In every person, the drive pedal is composed of three things—three P's—our:

1. Pain

2. People

3. Passion

All our motivation—our drive—comes from these three areas in our lives. The challenge is that most people have not adequately explored these three internal sources of drive, much less used them as fuel for great personal achievement. Look at all three of those areas and feel the emotion there. Allow them to inspire drive within you. Lean into the emotion you feel. Use it! Drive will begin to well up in you. That is your edge.

> *"Passion or drive is what moves the vehicle of a fulfilled life."*
>
> **—Israelmore Ayivor**

Drive is written by R. D. Saunders

"Time is what we want most,
but what we use worst."

—William Penn

Enough

e·nough

[iˈnəf]

Determiner and pronoun

1. As much or as many as required

Adverb

1. To the required degree or extent (used after an adjective, adverb, or verb)

Exclamation

1. Used to express an impatient desire for the cessation of undesirable behavior or speech

I think that ever more often, we're searching for the most significant elements that we think will bring meaning and fulfillment to our lives. We all seem to spend a lifetime searching for happiness, contentment, and love. We look for these elements in our relationships, in our jobs, in our possessions, and in our achievements. And we always look for them somewhere out there, in the future...instead of right here, in this moment.

Over the years while helping people, I have realized that if you feel like that you aren't *enough* or that you don't have enough, then you'll try to find a way to compensate for it.

I spent the better part of my adult life trying to be, look, and feel significant. When I founded Discovery Church in Orlando several decades ago, I thought it was all about God. I thought it was all about my desire to please God and help God. I thought it was all about my desire to help other people. And guess what? It was about that. But it was also about something else. It was about the fact that I never felt like I was enough…and that I needed to prove to myself and others that I was significant. I spent several decades helping to build a very large church that impacted multitudes of people, but underneath much of the goodness of that, I was trying to self-manufacture something else: an identity of significance.

The manufacturing process involved with that eventually brought me to an embarrassing level of exhaustion that contributed to my making the worst decision of my life—until I woke up in a way I never had.

I recently read that Anne Hathaway, a well-known actress, was being interviewed about what it felt like to win the Academy Award for Best Actress several years ago for her role in the movie *Les Misérables*. She described how she had spent her whole life working hard, clawing hard to get to that stage. Only once she got there, what she was looking for wasn't there. It was a low moment of her life. It ended up not being enough of the experience she thought she needed.

You need to know that *true* significance comes from within. It is actually a gift that's already been given, is extremely fulfilling, and lasts forever. *False* significance comes from without. It is something that we try to manufacture…create…on our own. It is extremely dissatisfying, lasts for a brief period of time, and will *never be enough*.

The following are three primary areas in which we all struggle with "enough-ness."

74

1. Shame: "I'm not enough."

Every time we compare ourselves to anyone else, we end up either exaggerating who we are or diminishing who we are...and it will never be enough. There is nothing wrong with approval except when we are using it or tempted to use it to cover our engine of *shame*. What has helped transform me is the reality that *I'm lavishly loved just as I am*.

2. Fear: "I don't have enough."

How many times a day do you think, "I don't have enough of something I really need?" The primary temptation regarding fear is assets. Whenever we operate out of fear, we manifest it by needing more assets, such as these four F's:

- I need more finances.

- I need more food.

- I need more friends.

- I need more fun.

Yet each time we get more, we discover that we can never get enough. There is nothing wrong with assets like those just listed, except when we are using them or tempted to use them to cover our engine of fear.

What has helped transform me is the reality that *I have a sufficient supply of everything I need, for this day*.

3. Guilt: "I haven't done enough."

Something I have personally experienced and that we hear all the time is people feeling like they haven't lived up to their full potential. Who establishes the mark we need to reach?

It's a funny thing, the concept of "potential." When we reach what was the last notch of our fullest potential, the mark mysteriously moves, and we must reach for a whole new level.

Throughout most of my life, I've felt the tug of that imaginary stat sheet in the sky that would show I had done enough.

The primary temptation regarding guilt is achievement. Whenever we operate out of guilt, we manifest it by needing more achievement. There is nothing wrong with achievements, but when they're used to cover the engine of guilt, they will never be enough!

What has helped transform me is the reality that *I have a unique and meaningful purpose for my life that I'm contributing to this day.*

When was the last time you thought, said, or felt the following?

1. "I'm not enough…I need more."

2. "I don't have enough…I need more."

3. "I haven't done enough…I need more."

The reality of our lives is that we actually *don't* need more to be OK. We already have enough, if we just take the time to experience what we have this day—*that is enough.*

> *When you feel like that you aren't enough or that*
> *you don't have enough, then you'll try to find a*
> *way to compensate for it.*

Enough is written by David Loveless

"Failure is an event, not a person."

—Zig Ziglar

Failure

fail·ure

/ˈfālyər/

Noun

1. *Lack of success*

2. *The omission of expected or required action*

Perhaps one of humanity's biggest fears is the fear of *failure*. I mean, who likes to fail? Here is the reality: everyone fails at something, sometime. I love the Zig Ziglar quote, "Failure is an event, not a person."

The truth is, like everything, life is always a battle of the mind. If we fail in our minds, we fail in life. That realization alone is worth the price of admission. As I look over my life, I realize that I have actually learned way more after a failure than I have ever learned after a success. Failing...does not make me a failure!

So why do we fear or even hate failure so much? For me, I suppose it is my pride. I want people to like me, and if I am totally honest, I want them to be impressed that I am so amazing. Great things never come without some failures! To be honest, it is often through the failure that we discover the best way to do something.

Think about it. If Thomas Edison had been consumed with the fear of failure, we would still be living in darkness. If Henry Ford had given up, we would still be riding on horseback. If Alexander Graham Bell had given in to the clutches of failure, we would be spending less time staring at those small plastic things we call phones that now hold most of our lives captive.

Most scientists are wrong most of the time, and nearly all athletes fail most of their attempts at a goal, a hit, or a basket. The rate of failure and the heartbreak associated with it is part and parcel of our everyday lives. So why, then, do we take failure so hard? Because we forget that success is achieved through trying, and trying most often ends in failure.

Let's examine seven R's that can help lead you to success:

1. Realize that everyone has failed.

2. Recover quickly; you will have another chance.

3. Remember what you did wrong, and adjust for the next time.

4. Resist the excuses that will hold you back.

5. Re-engage with your newly realized experience from the last failure, and focus your drive to go for it one more time, with a greater understanding.

6. Relax. You have this. Do not let a past fall stop you from trying again.

7. Rejoice! You did not give up.

*"My great concern is not whether you have failed,
but whether you are content with your failure."*

—Abraham Lincoln

Failure is written by Dr. Michael Smalley

"Who says life is fair? Where is that written?"

—William Goldman, The Princess Bride

/fer/

Adjective

1. *In accordance with the rules or standards; legitimate*

2. *(Of hair or complexion) Light; blond*

Adverb

1. *Without cheating or trying to achieve unjust advantage*

Noun (Archaic)

1. *A beautiful woman*

Verb (Dialect)

1. *(Of the weather) Become fine*

A more convoluted word you cannot find in our English language than *fair*. This word has been used as a crutch, an excuse, a verbal patsy. We don't reach higher to elevate ourselves or seek to be more than F**R.

In my mind, it is my "F" word. A word whose status is found with other slang and abusive words of scorn. A word that maybe at one time had real meaning, real honor, but now burns my ears like the foulest derogatory epitome of fear and misdirection.

You will find this "F" word on the lips of those living in mediocrity, looking for an excuse for why they don't reach higher. Why they got a bad rap or a bad deal. Why someone didn't treat them well or why they lost a race. They make statements like, "They won because the rules were not fair" or "I didn't do well because the rules were unfairly stacked against me." Excuses for life like, "Today you don't get a fair deal if you're not a _____ (fill in your blank)." Justifications often are stated as, "I was not treated fairly, so I now have the moral right to _____." So you act badly with perceived moral high ground because fair play is the new moral standard.

After all, an OK day is a fair day, an OK deal is a fair deal, and an OK day's pay is a fair amount. Yet we complain in a very nonspecific way that things are not fair, life is not fair, they were not fair, God is not fair. All of this in a lazy, noncommittal throw-out-the-"F"-bomb kind of way because we are not willing or able to address the true reasons why we don't self-elevate.

Really, the use of any slang or derogatory word is based on a lack of vocabulary. People often get lazy or uninspired, lose faith, walk away from God, or begin the slippery slope of blaming others for their current state. It becomes easier to throw the "F" word in than to have lively debate, have our ideas challenged, or hold ourselves to a higher standard. When we don't quite know what to say, we just revert to the empty and inappropriate "F" word.

Wouldn't it be great if we could build a legacy in our lives of not using the "F" word? Encourage our friends not to drop "F" bombs anymore? Help our children and grandchildren see how profane it is and encourage them to build a better vocabulary? Maybe even make it a game to pick better and more appropriate words instead of using that old and tired "F" word. Maybe it is time for some good old *word-replacement therapy*. Here are five steps to lose the "F" word:

1. Listen carefully for when you are about to use the "F" word, *fair*.

2. Stop yourself when you are about to drop an "F" bomb, and pause to

reflect on a better word.

3. Come up with a list of synonyms that really mean what you are feeling or thinking.

4. Take the time to look for ways to work these new, more meaningful words into your daily speech.

5. Help your friends and family see the emptiness of the word *fair*, and encourage them to practice word-replacement therapy, too.

You will begin to have higher thoughts with more meaning when you remove the "F" word daily:

1. Instead of trying to treat others *fairly*, I will endeavor to honor those around me with *respect* and *kindness*.

2. Instead of trying to give this task a *fair* shake, I will give this task my *level* best.

3. Instead of making a *fair* deal, I will now make *equitable* deals.

4. Instead of exhibiting *fair* play, I will play *justly* and *according to the rules*.

5. When I am not treated *fairly*, I will own my mess and understand that everyone is not *unbiased*.

6. Instead of saying the world is not *fair*, I will recognize what I can do to help the world become just, equitable, honest, upright, honorable, trustworthy, impartial, unbiased, objective, legitimate, reasonable, respectable, and acceptable—not *fair*.

"I looked up fairness in the dictionary, and it was not there."

—William Giraldi

Fair is written by AC Lockyer

"It is not death that a man should fear, but he should fear never beginning to live."

—Marcus Aurelius

/ˈfir/

Noun

1. *An unpleasant emotion caused by the belief that someone or something is dangerous, likely to cause pain, or a threat*

Verb

1. *Be afraid of (someone or something) as likely to be dangerous, painful, or threatening*

Ah, yes, *fear*. Life's greatest self-immobilizer. The heaviest shoes most people ever wear are made out of fear. They are laced up nice and tight to where they can't run, they can't walk, and heck, they can't even get a decent shuffle going.

And where is it people want to go that fear keeps them in a stationary place? Why, forward, of course. Forward toward a dream career, new or better relationships, a physical goal, or perhaps to quite simply escape an uncomfortable life situation.

What about your specific dreams? What is something you have thought of time and again when you play the Wish Game with yourself? You know the "Wish Game," right? During your morning ride into work, when your thoughts always seem to drift into a vision of you realizing a dream and saying, "Oh, how awesome would it be if I could just find a way to someday achieve (***insert dream here***)."

Now that you've identified your dream, it is purely yours to continue to hold onto and own. Don't let it go simply because fear has time and again gotten the best of you. You are not any different from every other human on this great planet who battles with this four-letter word.

I am a health coach, and people come to me for help in learning how to transform to a fit and healthy lifestyle. They can achieve this by participating in virtual group programs I facilitate throughout the year. One day, my friend, Emily, came to me very excited to get into one of my programs. She had even convinced a few of her business customers and friends to join the program as well. According to Emily, everyone was gung-ho and full of a high-five mentality about taking control of their weight-loss goals together.

As we were approaching the start date of the group program, I received a call from Emily. She gloomily told me that she and her friends had to back out of the program. When I asked why, she explained that the ladies who had originally committed to participate started to get nervous.

"Nervous?" I asked.

"Well, they were afraid that if they started, they might fail, and they didn't want that pressure on themselves," she responded.

While Emily's answer made me raise my eyebrows and shake my head in disbelief, I had to accept that this is the epitome of how fear works on people. Trust me. I know firsthand. I am never one to judge because I also played that same fear game with myself for more than a decade as I battled my own health and obesity issues. Instead of fulfilling a desire to get healthier and feel better about myself, I, like those ladies, allowed fear to, time and again, control my decision to not do anything. At nearly fifty pounds more than my current weight, for much of my life I remained unhappy with how I felt and looked. But I finally overcame this fear to commit to myself. Now I am in the best shape of my life.

Where many people can relate to this same type of hesitancy is in their jobs and careers. According to "Mind the Workplace," a joint study by the Faas Foundation and Mental Health America, 71 percent of employees are so dissatisfied with their workplace that they are considering or actively looking for new jobs. But just because many of these workers are unhappy does not mean they leave their employers. Why? Because of fear. Fear to leave a consistent paycheck and health benefits. Fear that they could go to another company and be inadequate compared to where they are now.

An even better example is for those want-to-be entrepreneurs. According to a survey released by the University of Phoenix Business School, close to 40 percent of employed workers want to start their own business. Many people are afraid to take this step because of how they might be viewed by other people with their business choice, or judged if they fail. I battled with this same fear as well when it came to my decision to start a side health-coaching business as a virtual coach.

This is a people business, and to me, that meant putting who the real Paul Perrino was out there on social media for people to see, trust, and engage with. In doing so, I was afraid of the judgment that would come from my family, friends, and people who did not even know me. It took well over a year for me to take that initial and very uncomfortable step, and the response has been tremendous. The fulfillment I get in helping others, the inspiration people tell me I have brought to their lives, and knowing that I finally have a business I can call my own has been a dream that was decades in the making.

Now back to your dream from the Wish Game. Perhaps your personal fears, and an unknown in how to overcome them, have made you simply carry your dream for years and years. So long indeed that your dream is becoming too heavy to hold, and you are thinking of dropping it altogether. Don't give up. I believe everyone has the ability to overcome their fear with a bit of direction and a positive push.

How do you start? Try "doing the A's," as follows:

1. **Do Ask.** While information is abundant and easily available on the internet and in books, there is no better way to complement your knowledge than by getting a mentor who understands your dream or goal. A mentor has been through the hard roads to achieve success and can help assuage your fears of the unknown.

2. **Do Act.** You can have all the know-how and book smarts on a subject, but until you take action and movement toward your goals, fear can creep in and build up a wall. Action equals confidence in your ability to continue moving in the right direction.

3. **Do it Again (and again, and again).** Unless you're among the small percentage of lucky ones who achieve their goals quickly, then welcome to the club with the rest of us, and be prepared to have setbacks. Many people who hit a bump in the road tend to quit because doubt creeps in, and when doubt creeps in, so does fear's ugly head. You have already built the courage to act, so use it to push through.

4. **Do it Authentically.** Remember, this is your dream or goal, and you should get fulfillment by being true to yourself. Do what feels right, and don't allow fear to limit this emotion.

5. **Do Achieve.** You can and you will. Stay strong with these actions, and one day you will look back to say, "What was I so afraid of?"

Don't let fear keep you from never beginning to live. The heavy pain in your stomach is nothing but regret caused by fear. Make the decision to push through fear, and a full heart and soul will be a result of your courage to live your life and dreams. Fear not, my friend, and you can and will achieve.

"Too many of us are not living our dreams because we are living our fears."

—Les Brown

Fear is written by Paul Perrino

"Leadership requires a nonstop demand of fortitude from Day 1 to the end."

—Bill Hybels

Fortitude

for·ti·tude

/ˈfôrdəˌt(y)o͞od/

Noun

1. Courage in pain or adversity

What is the one thing that separates success from failure? Why do some businesses fail while others excel? In a word, *fortitude*. In spite of skill, education, talent, or desire, success evades all who do not have the fortitude to see success through to fruition.

I have interviewed many candidates for new and challenging job assignments. As candidates deliver their résumés of accomplishments, it is amazing to witness that one special something that makes a leader choose a less educated candidate over a candidate who is clearly more educated. It's that spark of confidence and surety that speaks volumes about the probable success of a candidate, even before the discussion about specifics of the assignment they are being interviewed for takes place.

Successful leaders surround themselves with people who have the one common quality of all successful leaders: *strength in the face of adversity or difficulty*. Not the most educated or the most skilled, but the one with the fortitude to succeed in the face of impossibilities.

Another interesting aspect about the word itself is that it begins with "fort," defined as a "fortified building or strategic position." Then notice the second part of the word, "itude." It makes me think of the word "attitude." Maybe a proper definition of *fortitude* is "a strategic place of attitude to keep going, to not give up."

I have learned that everything is impossible until it is done just once. I remember hearing about a historic event that occurred on May 6, 1954. Paced by his friends, Chris Brasher and Chris Chataway, a twenty-five-year-old medical student named Roger Bannister ran a mile in 3:59.4 on the Iffley Road Track in Oxford, England, becoming the first human to run a sub four-minute mile. Since then, more than five hundred people have accomplished the "impossible," including five high school students.

Here's how to identify future leaders who will help you solidify success:

1. Find people who are *daring*—people who dare to do what others are afraid to do.

2. Hire people who are *destined*—people who are driven by a destiny for greatness.

3. Embrace people who are *dedicated* to your common goals.

4. Surround yourself with people who are *devoted* to you.

5. Employ people who will not be *denied* victory.

"Fortitude creates winners and champions that aren't always perfect but perfectly persistent."

—Allene Vanoirschot, *Daddy's Little Girl*

Fortitude is written by Wes Harris

"It is not the critic who counts; not the man who points out how the strong man stumbles, or where the doer of deeds could have done them better. The credit belongs to the man who is actually in the arena, whose face is marred by dust and sweat and blood; who strives valiantly; who errs, who comes short again and again, because there is no effort without error and shortcoming; but who does actually strive to do the deeds; who knows great enthusiasms, the great devotions; who spends himself in a worthy cause; who at the best knows in the end the triumph of high achievement, and who at the worst, if he fails, at least fails while daring greatly, so that his place shall never be with those cold and timid souls who neither know victory nor defeat."

—Theodore Roosevelt

/grit/

Noun

1. *Small, loose particles of stone or sand*

2. *Courage and resolve; strength of character*

Verb

1. *Move with or make a grating sound*

Life's journey is funny at times. I don't mean the kind of funny that makes you laugh, but the kind of funny that causes you to look deep inside yourself and ask, "How did I ever get through all that?"

I look back at my almost twenty-eight years as a Navy SEAL and wonder about all the challenges I faced. I look at persevering in Basic Underwater Demolition/SEAL training, where the attrition rate was close to 80 percent. I look at the 180 I made to become the husband and father my wife and daughter deserve. I reflect on how I went through multiple neck surgeries that included titanium implants, fusions, missing vertebrae, and a mild stroke that forced an earlier-than-expected retirement.

I see my transition from a high point in life, where I was once on top of the world as an elite warrior, to being a lost, dark soul barely able to pick up thirty pounds without my back going out. Fighting to regain a sense of purpose greater than myself. Using the available time to press a four-year doctoral program into three years.

So back to the question: "How did I ever get through all that?" The answer is found in an internal resolve, strength of will, moral fiber, more commonly known as *grit*!

For a majority of people, grit might initiate romantic images of cowboys and folks traveling across the great lands, headed west for a new life, or a poor athlete growing up in the projects who finds his way into the pros, or a dramatic scene of a soldier in a war movie, or a young, single mother bettering herself and making a good life for herself and her children.

Few would have imagery of themselves having grit. It is a fact that each of us is uniquely and wonderfully made, and that includes grit. It's a deep-seated resolve and internal fortitude that propels us through any challenge we might face.

The question is not whether someone has grit or not. The question is, will that person exercise it, develop it, and cultivate it into a personal strength? How do people allow their grit to drive them well beyond any destination they could have dreamed of?

Grit is forged in the fires of experience over time. The formula for grit looks like this:

Grit = Forged in the Fires of Experience

Time

Experiences are a magnificent teacher. The type of experiences I am referring to here are ones that involved a high level of challenge, as well as physical and mental discomfort, and resulted in some type of internal growth. The objective going forward is to squeeze the very most we can from each experience and avoid having to be painfully taught something specific more than once.

Also, we have to recognize how precious a commodity time really is. No one knows how much they have, and once spent, time can never be gotten back. To grow and develop your grit takes a high level of intentionality and personal investment. Here are three strategies those seeking a higher degree of grit can focus on:

1. Embrace the suck!

Grit is inherently about being comfortable being uncomfortable. Many people have assumed that my time on the SEAL Teams conditioned me to the harshness of cold. Absolutely not! What I learned from being on the teams was to suffer in silence and not whine about it, in addition to pursuing a way to get warm. You have to be willing to pursue what it takes to be successful, even in the most difficult of times.

2. Create a vivid picture of the future!

Creating a vivid picture of the future provides the needed focus for visualization while enduring the stressors that come with being forged by the fires of experience.

A vivid picture of the future has a high amount of preciseness and detail to promote goal development. I pursued each level of my education (undergraduate, graduate, and doctoral program) with a vivid picture of completing the requirements with the highest grades possible while maintaining life balance as a husband, a father, and a professional at work. Without a vivid picture of where I was headed, I would have been lost.

3. Develop and maintain a genuine reality!

Grit is not grounded in a fairy tale. An inaccurate or false sense of where you are is a disaster waiting to happen.

Imagine, if you will, a ship leaving port. The crew begins the journey from a known point and assesses their situation along the way until they reach their destination. The ship's crew constantly gathers information to develop a true reality of where they are on the chart. Assumptions won't work. Assumptions increase the cone of error and the probability of missing their destination. The only way to minimize that cone of error is to be guided by *truth*. Truth is not always easy to hear, but it's necessary if we are to have a genuine self-awareness of our abilities, competencies, and skills.

Grit is forged in the fires of experience over time. Embracing the suck, creating a vivid picture of the future, and developing and maintaining a genuine reality are three ways to reach a higher degree of grit in the challenges that life will present to you. Try one at first, and then exercise each of your grit muscles over time!

Developing grit that is forged through the fires of experiences over time requires intentionality and personal investment. No one—I mean *no one*—develops grit from the couch. Is it worth the gamble to live life like you're not going to die? What do you want to model for those who mean the most to you? What do others see—couch or grit? Take a long hard look in the mirror! What do you want to see?

> *"True grit is making a decision and standing by it, doing what must be done. No moral man can have peace of mind if he leaves undone what he knows he should have done."*

> **—John Wayne**

Grit is written by Dr. Chris Auger, BCC, LCDR (Ret.)

"Everyone needs someone to go to."

—Anonymous

Guide

guide

/gīd/

Noun

1. *A person who advises or shows the way to others*

2. *A structure or marking which directs the motion or positioning of something*

Verb

1. *Show or indicate the way to (someone)*

2. *Direct or have an influence on the course of action of (someone or something)*

The leader takes on a number of different roles on his or her path. Here are a few that come to mind: coach, visionary, mentor, and manager.

One description of a leader that I have come to embrace is that of a *guide*. This idea is functional with respect to an individual taking on the primary responsibility to help communicate and demonstrate the way forward, whether with direct reports or sales relationships. What if we could position ourselves in a more guide-like way when appropriate?

Recently, I took a call from a friend who has started a consulting business and is doing very well. He was eager to tell me about the success he had been having while pitching me on his services pretty aggressively. Every now and then, he would interrupt himself to assure me he was not attempting to sell anything. Had he asked me about my current projects, he would have captured my interest much sooner than he did. And he eventually did. He finally listened well enough and long enough to hear what's on my mind as we fire into the year's first quarter. Once I familiarized him with my current work narrative, he changed his approach and began to guide me toward a possible solution. As opposed to pitching his business, he sidled up next to me and became my ally. It felt totally different.

Luke had Yoda. Batman had Alfred. The Karate Kid had Mr. Miyagi. Everyone needs someone to go to. In most storylines, the hero needs a guide. Great parents do this. They listen. They guide their children.

I have noticed great people don't have perfect parents. In fact, my unofficial, undocumented research has reported that households with the "perfect" mom or dad seemed to live at the apex of dysfunction and sustain it well into adulthood. Really great parents who produce healthy, well-adjusted children all the way into adulthood listen well and are committed to guiding their offspring through life. They are not experts; they're just honest, vulnerable, and anything but perfect. They are the ones most likely to get phone calls and dinner invitations from their grown children. You've probably made the connection by now; leading is much like parenting, and the parent isn't the hero. He or she is just the guide.

Listen. What our teams, customers, and friends need from us will become clear as we listen.

Lose the desire to be a hero if you aspire to be a great guide.

Lean on someone as your guide.

"All you need to do to receive guidance is to ask for it and then listen."

—Sanaya Roman

Guide is written by Edgar Cabello

"The most beautiful things in the world cannot be seen or even touched; they must be felt with the heart."

—Helen Keller

/härt/

Noun

1. *A hollow muscular organ that pumps the blood through the circulatory system by rhythmic contraction and dilation. In vertebrates there may be up to four chambers (as in humans), with two atria and two ventricles*

2. *The central or innermost part of something*

Verb (Informal)

1. *Like very much; love*

I am committed to helping sales professionals be true to who they are, and I now dedicate every breath to doing so. Heart is greatly misunderstood. *Heart* is relevant in sales, culture, and leadership, yet so many seem to get it wrong.

Getting to the heart of the matter, if you are unable to uncover a personal or emotional need for prospects to make a change, then you might consider breaking off the meeting, thanking them for their time, and moving on to the next prospect.

Yes, I know it may be harsh. But all too often, those of us in sales will continue down the journey without finding what motivates the prospect to buy and then wonder why we can't close the sale.

It's not your motivation to sell; it's their motivation to buy.

Turn to your heart. Too many times, in sales especially, heart is ignored. "Heart-based" sounds "touchy-feely." "Heart-based" sounds weak and not cool. One's heart gets caged because, unfortunately, hard-core metrics still rule the sales roost.

I challenge you to learn to lead from the heart. Heart is about place and comfort. We are in a place to make a difference. We exhibit this in how we care for the people we work with. By living and leading with the heart, we create meaningful and unbreakable bonds that last a lifetime.

Heartfelt sales professionals are leaders: they build relationships, cast vision, and motivate people to take action.

It's about having the heart to rise up.

Real change in sales results starts with the heart. We need to peel away the layers of sales tactics to get to the root issues of the heart. This is where true motivation comes from. Tactics are OK, but to effect real change, we need to get to the heart of the matter.

Heart is the center of our being. We all seek more meaning and purpose in our *personal* lives, but few know how to connect this in our *sales* lives. Getting your heart right will ensure a long and fulfilling sales career.

If you are your authentic self, you have no competition.

A *selling from the heart* professional gets to root issues of the heart: authenticity, beliefs, and values. Authenticity in a world full of sales fakes and being genuine with follow-through is sorely lacking within the sales community.

Authenticity is one of the biggest challenges for salespeople in a profession riddled with unscrupulous, fake, and disingenuous sales reps. Quite frankly, many buyers despise them. Authenticity separates sales reps from sales professionals, and this is what buyers want!

It's about moving from being seen as untrustworthy to being seen as authentic and genuine. Yes, you must become a bit vulnerable with yourself because this is where it starts. To build relationships and change the way people think, you need to understand who you are and what goods you bring to the table.

Authenticity requires self-knowledge and self-awareness. Selling from the heart professionals accept their strengths and weaknesses. They're accountable to themselves. They're connected to their values and desires. They act deliberately in ways consistent with those qualities.

Selling from the heart professionals have sincere belief in themselves. They're comfortable in their own skin and don't pretend to be someone they're not. They understand who they are because they have an authentic sense of themselves. They encourage themselves to be themselves. And believing in themselves sets them apart from all others in sales.

To succeed in sales, we must understand that by just being ourselves, we're good enough to be great. By being ourselves, we believe in our ability to succeed. This automatically sets us apart from all of the other sales reps, who often just show up, throw up, and fail to ask heartfelt questions.

A true professional understands it is not about being different in your sales life than you are in your personal life. It's about congruence. It's about your alignment of your actions with the genuine, authentic, and real-deal version of you.

Know thy value, know thyself.

True professionals dedicate themselves to the sales profession. They add value because they understand their value. It's about the value they bring to the business table. They know what makes them different than all the other sales reps in their marketplace.

They understand the alignment of values. They understand and do the right things for the right reasons. They take the time to really understand their clients, their goals, and their initiatives. They do this because they care. Plain and simple, at the core of a selling from the heart professional lies one word: *care*!

It's imperative that sales professionals marry their value, their clients' value, and their companies' value in complete harmony to promote growth and better business.

Heart is a place where one develops and gains strength. Sales reps who embrace their focus on heart will grow in purpose, profit, and impact. Sales reps who embrace heart will strengthen their client relationships with many stakeholders, producing long-lasting results.

Your clients and prospects crave a genuine, authentic, real-deal and *selling from the heart* professional. I urge you to lead a sales life full of authenticity and integrity.

Actions speak louder than words when serving with the heart.

Here are five S's to help you bring your heart to the table:

1. **Sincerity**—Mean what you say, or don't say it. Live it, breathe it, and mean it.

2. **Substance**—Bring the best version of yourself by constantly working on yourself.

3. **Soul**—Without a heart, you have no soul.

4. **Simplicity**—Don't overcomplicate sales. Look to build meaningful and credible relationships.

5. **Share**—Get out there and share yourself, your heart, and how you can help. Without a beating heart, how can you share the best version of you?

Sincerity + substance + heart will set you apart.

Heart is written by Larry Levine

"We must accept finite disappointment, but never lose infinite hope."

Dr. Martin Luther King, Jr.

/hōp/

Noun

1. *A feeling of expectation and desire for a certain thing to happen*

2. *(Archaic) A feeling of trust*

Verb

1. *Want something to happen or be the case*

I watched a vibrant, healthy, beautiful young girl slip into motionless, emotionless existence. Unable to get out of her bed, the light in her eyes and the spark in her soul grew dim. She had no desire, no ability, to get up, wash her face, comb her hair, or face the day. She had slipped into a dark coma of depression. That's what hopelessness does.

When your mind says, "give up," *hope* whispers, "one more try." At any given moment, you have the power to say, "This is not how the story is going to end."

Hope is the anticipation that something good is going to happen. You might have had a setback, but now it's time for a comeback!

You might not realize it until it's gone, but hope fuels your life. Like a fully functioning automobile that's out of gas, you have all the faculties, all the potential in the world for greatness. You can achieve, you can accomplish, and you can effect change. You can move, motivate, and manage. You have a phenomenal capacity to make this world a better place—and enjoy yourself doing it!

Ah, but an essential ingredient for any of this to happen is that you must have hope. Hope is the fuel in your soul tank. Hope gives you something to look forward to. Hope gives you a reason to get up in the morning. Maybe it's something as simple as hoping to enjoy a date this Friday with your spouse—or someone you secretly hope one day may be your spouse. Maybe it's hoping you will pass your exam, get a raise, or watch your son play his first game of T-ball. Perhaps you are new in town and hope to make a new friend. The more things you have to hope for, the brighter your day will be.

We talk a lot about love, persistence, faith, diligence, trustworthiness, wisdom, and knowledge—all the things we should seek. All things that we both pursue and display. Yet without hope, we will accomplish none of these things. Hope is essential. We can live on *diminished* hope just like we can get along with less food, less opportunity, or less comfort. But take away *all* hope, and we die.

So what can you do to stir up hope? If you want to inspire hope in others, you have to be hopeful yourself. You can't give away what you don't have. The good news is, hope is contagious. Have a positive outlook. Constantly comment on the potential that lies just around the corner. If you are the person who focuses on what's possible, if your glass is always half full, that affects people around you.

You want to change the world? Start changing the world around you by speaking words of hope. Speaking is important. You can have hope in your heart that fuels you. But when you speak words of expectation and affirmation, when you speak about what's possible, you are changing the atmosphere.

Hope is *believing* that circumstances will be better. It's not *wishing* that things will get better, but an actual belief, even when there may be no evidence that anything will change. Hope can encompass a wide variety of beliefs—hoping for a reconciliation, hoping for safe arrival, a patient hoping to be healed from cancer. Hope is like a muscle: the more you work at it, the stronger it gets! Don't ever lose hope.

Even within the darkest circumstances of my life—loss of loved ones, divorce, betrayal, and financial disasters—there are rays of hope that can illuminate that darkness.

When you face dark circumstances, be an agent of hope. Make a "Hope List" of things you are looking forward to. If you are having trouble coming up with anything to put on your list, invite a friend or two to help you. Sometimes, if your own hope light is too dim, you lose sight of your own positive potential. There's no shame in asking others to help you identify things you can look forward to, things that will inspire fresh hope in your heart. Then, as your own hope quotient rises, be the person who speaks about the good that's possible. Your positive confession, your hopeful commentary, will increase your leadership influence as you positively affect those around you.

Don't let adversity break you. Instead make it the motivation you need to go on in life. Walk with hope in your heart, and you'll never walk alone.

"Man can live about forty days without food, about three days without water, about eight minutes without air... but only for one second without hope."

—Hal Lindsey

O—m

Hope is written by Marc Mero

"Genius is in the idea. Impact, however, comes from action."

—Simon Sinek

Noun

/ˈimˌpakt/

1. The action of one object coming forcibly into contact with another

Verb

1. Come into forcible contact with another object

2. Have a strong effect on someone or something

I will never forget having the honor of speaking at my dad's funeral. Looking out at the large gathering, I realized that over his long life, he made a positive *impact* on the world. He was not wealthy, nor was he a prominent leader. Yet those of us who spoke of him, from his children to his friends to people who knew him from a distance, all talked about the incredible impact he had on our lives.

What kind of impact will you make? To live a life with impact, you must sustain positive momentum, manage your resources, and focus your life.

1. Sustain Positive Momentum

To live a life with impact, you need the power that comes from momentum. Like the freight train that slowly gathers speed, a person of impact creates sustained momentum through positive action. "What you do has far greater impact than what you say," remarks Stephen Covey. Each positive action is like a shovel full of coal that fuels the boiler of a steam engine.

Momentum isn't created in a day, a week, or even a month. Momentum is created over years and even decades of positive actions. You create momentum to impact individuals when you take positive action to invest in others. My small action today to spend time encouraging someone leaves a mark on that person's life.

Your small choice today to do something seemingly small, like writing an article or drafting a proposal, might seem insignificant. However, every world-changing company, product, book, and revolution was birthed through positive action. The sum of many small actions creates momentum that impacts your family, friends, coworkers, and everyone you encounter.

2. Manage Your Resources

To make a positive impact, you must also manage your resources, directing them toward the areas you want to impact. Each person has three resources that can be managed: time, energy, and money.

Time—To make a positive impact, you need to allocate your time strategically. Time is our most sacred resource. Author and mega-church pastor Bill Hybels says, "Next to the Bible, your calendar is your most sacred document." How much attention do you give each day to allocating your time? Do you allow enough margin to impact people?

Energy—To make a positive impact, you need energy. Physical energy comes from a healthy diet, exercise, and good sleep habits. Mental energy comes from reading. Emotional energy comes from friendships and hobbies. Spiritual energy comes from meditation, reflection, prayer, and worship. How much attention do you give to creating and sustaining energy

Money—To make a positive impact, you need financial resources. It's not the amount of money you have. Instead, have you arranged your finances in a way that allows you the freedom you need to make an impact? This involves creating a sustainable lifestyle that minimizes the amount of time you have to work to "keep the lights on" and allows you the margin you need to impact the world. What could you do to reduce overhead expenses and increase recurring income to create more financial margin?

3. Focus Your Life

To make a big impact, you also need to focus your life. What is the story of your life? What makes your heart come alive? Where are you in your journey? Ask yourself these types of questions on a regular basis. People of impact intentionally focus their lives on what matters.

Years ago, a wise leader shared his strategy of taking quarterly sabbaticals. I've sustained this habit for nine years, and it has changed my life. During three days off the grid, I reconnect with my goals, reflect on what I've accomplished, and plan the next ninety days.

My focus continues in weekly and daily habits. Each weekend, I take an hour to reconnect with my quarterly plan, review the previous week, and plan the next one. Daily, I take fifteen minutes to remember my weekly plan, review the previous day, and plan my current day. This focuses my energy on my priorities.

What impact will you make?

Impact happens when you sustain momentum with positive choices, manage your resources, and focus your life. Someday your child will

speak at your funeral. What will he or she say about the impact you had on your family and on the world?

Impact is written Darrell Amy

"Inspiration exists, but you have to find it working."

—Pablo Picasso

/inˈspī(ə)r/

Verb

1. *Fill (someone) with the urge or ability to do or feel something, especially to do something creative*

2. *Breathe in (air); inhale*

We live in a world bombarded with distraction and obsessed with measuring talent and performance. This is why it is so easy to forget the *fundamental* role of inspiration in our lives. Inspiration awakens us and drives us to new possibilities to transcend our ordinary limitations. Inspiration is the necessary ingredient to put an end to apathy and move on to the possibility of what can become.

Many times, when we hear the word "inspiration," we overlook it because of its association with something supernatural or divine. However, the latest research shows that inspiration can be activated, captured, and used to have a transcendental impact on our lives and legacies.

The truth is this: *all great success stories start with inspiration.* Even projects, businesses, or achievements that aren't that great originally start with some sort of inspirational thought, even if the eventual outcome bears little resemblance to that original light-bulb spark of creativity.

Of course, long-term success depends on much more than sheer inspiration. Thomas Edison maintained, "Genius is 1 percent inspiration and 99 percent perspiration," and he certainly had a point. Looked at another way, this equation just underlines the fact that when it comes to achieving outstanding results, 100 percent perspiration is just not going to do it, even though it seems to be the strategy of choice for many business leaders.

For years, I have been fascinated with the word *inspire*. Not only do I have it as the license plate on my car, it is also written and displayed in different decorations and arrangements inside my house. Moreover, my wife and I decided to name our company Inspire International because of the power this word connotes in our lives and in what we do every day.

The word *inspire* translates to "*in spirit.*" Inspiration comes from within.

The word "inspiration" denotes thoughts or emotions associated with things that lead us to take action. However, *inspiration* has a much deeper connotation. The root of the word *inspiration* can be traced back to the Latin *inspirare* ("to breathe or blow into"), which is from the word *spirare*, meaning "to breathe."

Some people watch hundreds of motivational videos, looking for inspiration. Tech entrepreneurs visit the latest technological advances every few hours, looking for new inspiration. Musicians, writers, artists, and everyone else all scour the world for inspiration. Yet most of them aren't feeling inspired enough. They're looking for more, thinking something else out there will truly inspire them. Why is this? Because nothing is truly inspiring unless you apply it to your work and life. ("Work" means your life's output, whether creative, business, or personal.) In other words, your work itself is the inspiration. Everything created has been inspired.

You might hear something or see something that gives you a new idea. But it's only when you stop and think of your work through this new perspective that you actually take action and go turn the idea into reality. That's the real inspiration that everyone is looking for. Inspiration is not just receiving information.

Inspiration is taking action—applying what you've received. People think that if they keep reading articles, browsing books, listening to talks, or meeting people, they're going to suddenly get inspired. For every bit of inspiration you receive, use it and amplify it by *applying* it to your work. Then you'll finally feel the inspiration you've been looking for.

What inspires you? Remember, there is no inspiration if there is no action. Hence, the popular idea that artists work when their inspiration comes to them is terribly wrong and dangerous. If you are looking for inspiration and want to achieve long-lasting results, you must embrace the inspiration to propel you to take action immediately. Inspiration is a factor that can move mountains and change the direction of entire lives. It creates an energy and enthusiasm that are hard to extinguish and that can keep us going through the most difficult and challenging times to reach our goals. Inspired people are passionate leaders, and passion is the greatest motivator human beings experience.

Here are four I's—strategies you can follow to help you get inspired:

1. **Ignite.** Inspiration works through all three dimensions of our lives: spirit, soul, and body. The inspiration can be ignited when our spiritual dimension is connected to God.

2. **Ideas.** An idea is the product of inspiration. Whatever has been manifested as an inspirational thought came in the form of an idea in our conscious minds. On a daily basis, we must cultivate and protect our ideas

3. **Increase.** The most inspiring leaders understand the power of *increase* to get inspired. Increase your energy by eating well on a daily

basis. Increase the number of hours you spend doing what you love. Increase the quality of time you spend with your family. Increase your team with the right people who will work alongside you to make things happen, rather than issuing directives. Two of the most inspiring ways to increase are "we" and "together."

4. **Ignore.** To keep yourself inspired, you will have to learn how to ignore those thoughts, even people, that want to sabotage or kill your inspiration. The worst enemy of inspiration is to not know how and when to ignore what raises against your course of action.

Challenge yourself to become personally inspired. The best you can do is set up the optimal environment for inspiration. Take action, and let others be impacted by the impact of everything you do.

Inspire is written by Ronald Joselin

"Whoever is careless with the truth in small matters cannot be trusted with important matters."

—Albert Einstein

Integrity

in·teg·ri·ty

/inˈtegrədē/

Noun

1. *The quality of being honest and having strong moral principles; moral uprightness.*

2. *The state of being whole and undivided*

The root of the word *integrity* is "integer." In math, an integer is a whole number, as opposed to a fraction. So integrity represents a wholeness in life as opposed to being fractured or living a "partial" life.

A true sign of maturity and strength of character is to be the same person no matter where you are or who you're with. Integrity is who you are when no one is looking, when there is nobody around to impress. It is when your private life matches your public image. It's doing what you said you would do, keeping your promises.

Where does integrity come from? Are we born with it? Is it simply human nature or learned behavior?

I remember, as a young boy, going uptown with friends and visiting the Ben Franklin Five and Dime store. After looking at the magazines and comics, we would usually walk out with penny candy in our pockets that we didn't pay for. At that young age, we did not see penny theft as a big deal.

As I grew older, I remember going back to that same store with my father. He drove that five to ten minutes to return the ten cents that the sales clerk had overpaid him on an earlier purchase. That made quite an impression on me. I realized it wasn't about the money; it was about doing what was right!

I've come to the conclusion that integrity does not come easily or naturally. We all need people in our lives to model and teach us the importance of practicing integrity in every aspect of our lives. My dad was my master instructor, and I saw the fruits of his integrity play out over the years.

I realized it was my duty to model that same integrity to my daughter and others I influence. Does anybody come to *your* mind? Who is looking to you to be a model of integrity?

I'm reminded of the story of the salesman who was waiting to see the purchasing agent so he could submit his company's bid. While he was waiting, he couldn't help but notice that his competitor's bid was sitting on the purchasing agent's desk.

Unfortunately, the actual figure for the bid was covered by a drink can. He thought, "How could it hurt if I took just a quick look? No one would ever need to know." So he reached over and lifted the can. His heart sank as he watched hundreds of BB's pour out of the bottomless can and scatter across the desk and onto the floor.

It was a test that the purchasing agent had set up, and the salesman failed miserably. Needless to say, he didn't get that company's business.

You can *never* go wrong living a life of integrity. Unfortunately, it is way too easy to become oblivious to decisions we make each day that do not model that characteristic. It's an ongoing journey.

Stop for a minute and think about what integrity means to you as you walk through your workday.

For me, integrity means doing the following:

1. **Decide what is important to me and how I need to live my life.** Then, regardless of any applied pressure, continually honor my values. Effective living occurs once we make that decision.

2. **Commit myself to not agreeing to do things unless I'm going to follow through.** Even if I later feel the commitment doesn't justify my time, there is great value in just being trustworthy and following through.

3. **Live my life with the thought that my boss, my wife, my children, and my friends are watching me.** (Not to mention God!)

4. **Keep a confidence when asked. Be careful not to share that information with *anybody*.** (No, not "just this one time.")

I challenge you this week to be intentional in living a life of integrity. Consciously make decisions that show your commitment to do what you say you will, no matter who is around or what the consequences are.

I believe you will find reward through stronger relationships, strengthening of your self-worth and value, and peace, passion, and purpose that come from living a "whole" life.

Better is the poor who walks in his integrity than
one perverse in his ways, though he be rich.

—Proverbs 28:6 (NKJV)

Integrity is written by Terry Steen

/lēd/

Verb

1. *Cause (a person or animal) to go with one by holding them by the hand, a halter, a rope, etc. while moving forward*

2. *Be a route or means of access to a particular place or in a particular direction*

Noun

1. *The initiative in an action; an example for others to follow*

2. *A position of advantage in a contest; first place*

So many things are written, shared, and taught about leadership these days. In fact, I think the concept has become sadly overused, and perhaps misused. Let's break this definition down. The *word* lead can be a noun or a verb.

I was discussing this concept recently with my friend, Joe Calamusa IV, who heads the sales training program for the University of Alabama. He mentioned to me that as he travels the country training sales hopefuls, and interacting with major companies and their leaders, he has come to realize that that most people seem to be familiar with their attempt to embrace the *noun*, but few of us understand how to lead as the *verb*.

In other words, we are OK with showing people *what* to do and *where* to go, and we simply "hope" they follow. The *noun* form of the word puts all the reasonability in the hands of the follower, but the one who embraces the *verb* shares it. And in fact, the verb puts much reasonability on the one who is in the lead.

The first thing that jumps out to me is that to "lead" is to *cause*. When I am leading someone or something, I cause them to *do* such and such to *go* to some place. I actually create a force, if you will...not a force like you "have no choice" or I am "forcing you to," but more of a plan, a vision, a suggestion, that causes them to *want* to be a part of what I am doing or going where I am.

The second reality that jumps out at me is the idea that there needs to be a full, continual connection ("to go with someone by holding them by the hand") with the people we are attempting to lead. This cannot be accomplished by simply speaking to them. It cannot be achieved by pointing them in a certain direction. Even if the direction is right, we need to *lead* them.

When I was an executive, I had a management team who reported to me weekly. I was privileged to spent thirty minutes each week with every manager, and the first fifteen minutes were my favorite! You see, I would have them share with me from their lives. Not from their jobs. Not about a project, or a problem. No, we would talk about their kids or their hobbies. I would cry with them about a grandmother who just passed or rejoice with them about the discovery that they were expecting a child. You see, I was connected to them, and when I needed to lead them, they would tend to want to follow me because they knew I cared about them, and they knew I had their best interests in view.

Perhaps a good way to understand this better is to compare the difference between the person who leads by *pulling* with the one who attempts to lead by *pushing*.

You see, I can push you in any direction, but I do not have to be there... in fact, I usually am not. But if I pull you, I must bring you to the place I am. You come *by* me. I pull you *toward* me. With me. The picture is, I am in front, leading you. I think about when I was helping my children learn to walk. I did not push them. I did not give them a strong shove and say, "I sure hope you learn to walk soon, or you will bust your face when you fall..." No! I would hold them by the hand and walk in front of them as their example. I would bring them forward to do what they had not done and go where they had not gone without my assistance.

We can *push* people and barely touch them. But it is impossible to *pull* someone without total, continual contact. Another key comparison between push with pull is it that it is difficult to control the direction of a push. But when I pull someone, I can guide them exactly where they need to be. We can create a path of desired destiny.

The third reality that jumps out about this topic is the need to define *lead* correctly. I need to move people *forward*. Not just with movement, but a *forward* movement. If I truly lead you, then I should take you to a place you may never have gone without me. A place I have been, or at least a place I am willing to come back to, so I can bring you there, too.

Over the years, I have had the privilege and reasonability to lead others. I must admit that, far too often, especially in my younger years, I would push them and not pull them. But now, I want to personify the verb of *lead*. I will cause others to move forward because I am continually connected to them. I am willing to hold on to them until I help them get where they desire to go. By the way, I have people right now in my life holding my hand, too.

Here are the steps to lead others effectively:

L – *Leverage* your relationships.

E – Be the *example*.

A – *Associate* with those you are to lead and who are leading you.

D – Be *determined* to pull them forward.

"The greatest leader is not necessarily the one who does the greatest things. He is the one that gets the people to do the greatest things."

—Ronald Reagan

Lead is written by Chris Gingrasso

"Thoughts are real, physical things that occupy mental real estate. Moment by moment, every day, you are changing the structure of your brain through your thinking."

—Caroline Leaf, PhD

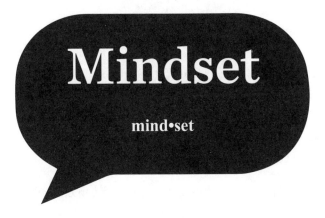

Mindset

mind•set

/ˈmīn(d)set/

Noun

1. *The established set of attitudes held by someone.*

I was standing on the sideline at football practice when one of our starters put his arm around my shoulders and said, "Doc, I've never thought so much about what I've been thinking about! I think I can really take my game to another level if I can choose the right thoughts at the right time and build *mindsets* that help me succeed."

What this young man was awakening to is the true power that lies within us as human beings: our minds. While the *brain* is the two- to three-pound mass in our heads, the *mind* is the discernment and choice aspect that makes us different than any other species. Although the brain is not a muscle in the scientific sense, it functions like a muscle in the sense that the parts of it that we use grow and get stronger, and the parts of it that we don't use get smaller and weaker.

Our thoughts literally change the form and function of our brains. As we repeat thoughts over and over, they begin to wire into the brain what we call *mindsets*, or patterned ways of thinking. These mindsets are literal protein patterns that get wired into the brain and begin impacting how we "show up" to every area of our lives.

We have mindsets about everything: who we are as leaders, what our family heritage says about us, how people with different backgrounds function, etc. Brain science reveals that 75 to 98 percent of all mental and physical health issues are caused due to our thought life and the mindsets we wire into our brains. It is critical that we start thinking about what we are thinking about so we can build mindsets that lead to health, peace, and consistent performance excellence, even when it's difficult.

The beautiful thing about thoughts is that we can control them! With so many variables in our lives that are out of our control, it should be encouraging to know that the biggest driver of our personal and professional success lies within our direct influence.

While we cannot always choose what thoughts pop into our heads, our minds can make the choice to hold on to those thoughts and allow them to build a mindset in our brains, or to release them and replace them with more helpful and productive thoughts. This is the power of the mind!

I started playing soccer when I was seven years old, and I had this one T-shirt that I loved. It read, "I am strong. Powerful. Equal. A threat. I am an athlete." Every time I put on that shirt—which was a lot, just ask my mom—I would repeat that phrase in my mind. Then I found myself starting to say it in my head on the field. It started to shape my game as I played up levels, against the boys, or even opponents who were technically better than I was. I truly started to believe that I was strong and powerful and equal and a threat, regardless of the situation or task at hand.

Let's fast-forward to my first year after graduating from Notre Dame with an undergraduate business degree. I found myself sitting around a board-room table and shrinking in my skin after being demeaned in front of the room by a colleague who found my contributions to the conversation irrelevant. My heart rate increased, and I remember thinking, "No. Sit up straight. Hold your head up. And remember, you are strong, powerful, equal, and a threat."

I had not worn my little shirt or thought of that statement in years, but suddenly, when my back was against the ropes and I was at a moment of choice to either lean into a hard moment or shrink into someone else's perception of who I was capable of being, it flashed through my brain. Unbeknownst to me at the time, that phrase had become a mindset. It was wired into my brain. And it impacted how I was able to "show up" in that moment: I sat up. I kept my eyes up. I forced myself to add another comment. And ten minutes later, when that man took my very comments and repackaged them into his own words to share with the group, I was reminded that I was strong, powerful, equal, and yes, perhaps even a threat.

This is the power of mindsets in our lives. We need to understand the mindsets that help us show up as the best version of ourselves and deliver consistent performance excellence. We also need to understand those mindsets that are actually hurting us by limiting our courage in the moment to show up and deliver.

Here are five R's to help you build mindsets that help position you to show up and deliver the best of who you are on a more consistent basis:

1. **Recognize**. Start thinking about what you are thinking about! It is only after you start to recognize your thoughts and the mindsets you have built over time that you will be able to build more productive ones.

2. **Replace**. If you recognize negative or unproductive ways of thinking, replace them with positive and more productive thought patterns.

3. **Repeat**. Write down at least three "power statements"—positive, powerful, productive ways of thinking about yourself, your mission, or your

team. And then repeat them every day until you wire them into your brain.

4. **Renovate**. Renovate your space! If your office, meeting room, or home doesn't help energize and reinforce the ways of thinking and being that you aspire to, change it! It will help expedite the development of healthier and more powerful mindsets.

5. **Rally**. Many of us need to stop *listening* to ourselves and start *talking* to ourselves. Use your words to rally your head, heart, and hands to deliver the very best you have in the moment. Pep talks aren't just for athletes; they're for all of us!

Mindsets make us. Choose today who you want to be and what you want to accomplish, and then build mindsets that transform you into that person!

"Successful people don't have any fewer problems than unsuccessful people; they just have a different mindset in dealing with them."
—John C. Maxwell

Mindset is written by Dr. Amber Selking

> *"Motivation has no power until it is pointed at your purpose."*
>
> **—Bishop TD Jakes**

Motivation

mo·ti·va·tion

/ˌmōdəˈvāSH(ə)n/

Noun

1. *The reason or reasons one has for acting or behaving in a particular way*

2. *The general desire or willingness of someone to do something*

The two definitions of the noun *motivation* tell the multifunctional story of this multifaceted word. I begin with the second: the general desire or willingness of someone to do something. That indicates that our desire is determined, at least in part, by something we've been asked or decided to do. Is there a cause and effect relationship between something and our desire to do it?

Sure. We have more motivation to tackle some tasks than others. Follow-up question: Could we be even more successful if our willingness to do something wasn't as influenced by the something itself? Sure. Take two tasks that equate in their contribution to our personal goals. One something comes with a higher natural general desire to complete. It is instinctively preferable over the less-desirable something. By definition, we'll be more motivated to accomplish the former. If we're more motivated to accomplish it, then it stands to reason that there is at least a slight probability that we'll pursue it with more energy and thoroughness than we will the less-preferable something.

So once we've completed both, our collective progress toward our personal goals is less than it would be if we have been equally motivated to complete these two equally important somethings.

That's when the first definition of the word takes its place in the pursuit of our purpose: the reason or reasons one has for acting or behaving in a certain way. This is not the same as the second definition. This definition implies an *external* stimulus that is independent from the general desire of someone to do something. This definition provides us with permission to locate an external power source to increase motivation *beyond* our natural willingness. We need that external power source, like a backup generator, to move us to complete the less-desirable task with the same intention and intensity as the something we naturally prefer.

Even the specificity of the definition is instructive: reason or reasons. So we could even combine external sources of motivation, if need be, to give us that extra boost of power when attacking the most difficult somethings. It doesn't matter if those reasons are intrinsic or extrinsic. It doesn't matter if they're intangible or tangible. It matters only that they motivate us to do our best when what we have to do would instinctively elicit less than that standard of behavior.

As I teach hundreds of students at The University of Alabama and thousands of professionals across corporate America, I find the same dividing line within each of those two diverse groups. Lines are easily drawn based on who resigns their daily regimen to their "general desire or willingness" versus those who seek the required reasons to "behave in a particular way." Those in the latter category excel because they're unwilling to let their own unwillingness stand in their way.

The following six strategies will help fuel your motivation:

M – Build your own motivation *matrix*.

O – *Offer*, but don't force, your motives on others.

T – Allow *time* to give you the courage to take risks.

I – Motivation is *inspiration* with staying power.

V – *Visualization* is a source of self-motivation.

E –Your *elevation* is a function of your motivation.

Here's a quote that captures the meaning and importance of motivation without even using the word:

> *"If you can't fly, then run. If you can't run, then walk. If you can't walk, then crawl, but by all means, keep moving."*
>
> **—Dr. Martin Luther King, Jr.**

Motivation is written by Joe Calamusa IV

*"If you cannot find peace within yourself, you
will never find it anywhere else."*

—Marvin Gaye

Peace

peace

/pēs/

Noun

1. *Freedom from disturbance; tranquility*

2. *A state or period in which there is no war or a war has ended*

If we only understood the power of the word *peace* and its importance in our lives. Unfortunately, most of us have a very shallow or superficial view of this word. We see it as someone just "tiptoeing through the daisies," as the great Tiny Tim used to sing. Or we associate it with people who are kind of flaky and detached from the real world who are not really engaged in real life but rather are living in their own alternative universe.

But that's not what real peace means at all. It's so much more than simply the absence of conflict or serenity. In fact, in biblical times, the Hebrew word for peace was *shalom*, and the Greek word was *eirene*. These words take on a whole new meaning and go a whole new level that can impact every area of our lives—in our relationships, our businesses, our finances, even our goals and dreams. The true meaning of *peace* can affect our decision-making process—how and why we make the decisions we're making.

True, genuine peace isn't just the absence of conflict; it's the result of something even better in its place. In other words, true peace means to be complete or whole. It's not just simply stopping a bloody mess, but replacing it with something that makes it even better than it was before. Restored to be more beneficial more valuable than it was in the past.

Shalom refers to a stone that has perfect shape with no cracks or a wall that has no gaps or missing pieces. It also refers to something that has complexity and perhaps many moving pieces but remains in a state of completeness or wholeness. In other words, it's complete—nothing is missing. As an example, to bring *shalom* to a broken relationship is more than simply the stopping of the fighting; rather, it's a healing so strong that two people actually start working for each other's own benefit, creating an even deeper, stronger bond.

Unfortunately, in my career, I've been around far too many businesses that are experiencing anything but *shalom*. When I first moved into the business community, I was under the impression that every businessman had his stuff together and knew all the ins and outs of running a business.

To my surprise, it's anything but that. I've found that most business owners (much like anything else in life) have no idea how to run a business. They know their skill sets and industries proficiently but have no idea how to build a business around it. Instead, what most do is just wing it and build it to a certain point that it just survives and limps along. Most of the time, that creates a life of stress, not only for themselves but for their staff members, as well as their families, who have to live with them through this process. In other words, their businesses run them rather than them running their business.

Some are so overwhelmed and stressed they don't even want to face or deal with the realities of what they've created or what it has evolved into. They don't have a clue what's really going on and many times are afraid to find out. Can you say "disaster?"

Let's be honest. What I've described is how most relationships get started. We have no idea what we're doing, but the dreams and fantasies of it sound so good. Then, in no time, bammm! The honeymoon phase is short-lived, and then reality raises its ugly head.

Is the concept of true *shalom* peace even realistic? Or is that just pie-in-the-sky thinking, and we just have to learn to suck it up and deal with the cards we're handed?

Well, I can honestly tell you with full and complete confidence that *shalom* is not only possible; it's expected. Think on that for a second: it's not simply an option or an opportunity, it's expected! And if you can approach your life with that type of attitude of "expectation," rather than simply sticking the proverbial toe in the water for a try-it-and-see approach, you'll be amazed at the results.

I've been so bold as to lay out some tips that I've learned over the years as a business owner, a father, and a friend. I've come to realize that truth is truth. It applies whether in business, with family, or with friends. People are people. No matter their role or function in our lives, the principles still work.

Here are the tips:

1. **Stop the bleeding now!** Don't wait till it's too late. The longer you wait, the weaker it becomes—to the point of either paralysis or even death being just around the corner.

2. **Burn the bridges.** Don't give yourself any other outs. Make the decision that it's do or die, sink or swim. Have an "I'm gonna make this happen one way or another" kind of determination.

3. **Be honest with yourself.** This is probably the biggest challenge of all. We love to play games with ourselves and allow ourselves to get distracted when it's convenient.

4. **Set aside the emotions.** We use emotions to discourage others, or in-

timidate them, or make them feel guilty so the truth bombs don't hurt so bad. Just take it! As the old Southern say'n goes, "Suck it up, buttercup."

5. **Be willing to listen.** This is one of the most underdeveloped and misunderstood skills, but I'm convinced it's one of the most powerful gifts anyone can have.

6. **Make the tough decisions.** The toughest are those that are not self-serving but are right.

7. **Be willing to make changes.** The biggest and most important come from inside.

Expect *shalom* to permeate every aspect of your life: marriage, family, friends, business, and most importantly, your relationship with God. You'll find that the last one is honestly the answer for all the others; it's the very essence of *shalom*....just say'n!

> *"Success isn't measured by money or power or social rank. Success is measured by your discipline and inner peace."*
>
> **—Mike Ditka**

Peace is written by Bradly Stroud

"Don't lower your expectations to meet your performance. Raise your level of performance to meet your expectations. Expect the best of yourself, and then do what is necessary to make it a reality."

—Ralph Marston

Performance

per·for·mance

/pərˈfôrməns/

Noun

1. *An act of staging or presenting a play, concert, or other form of entertainment*

2. *The action or process of carrying out or accomplishing an action, task, or function*

Peak performance. High performance. Horrible performance. Great performance. How many phrases with the word *performance* have you heard? *Performance* has become a buzz word. Ambitious individuals and athletes can't stop thinking about it. Growth-minded companies can't seem to operate without the latest gadget advertised to boost it.

The problem is, most people treat performance like a magic pill. "Do this performance technique, and you'll go to the next level." "Train your employees with these performance tactics, and your business with double its revenue." I hate to break it to ya, but there's no such thing as a magic, cookie-cutter performance pill.

Performance relies on *your* unique ability to *perform*. Noticeably, *perform* is the root word of *performance*, and it means to "carry into effect, fulfill, discharge."

Therefore, if you don't have the ability to perform, you won't be able to carry into effect anything at the level you want and will likely fall short of your ultimate goal. That raise you want...that business growth you set out to have...that championship you want to win...that deeper relationship you envisioned...

It's like the 150-pound teenage boy who has never lifted anything heavier than fifty pounds. He takes a steroid because he wants to match his peers' ability to lift a car. He could pop the pill, but that car still ain't movin' because he doesn't have the ability to lift it!

Let me say this again—because most don't get it the first time. Your *performance* relies on your *ability* to perform.

So, how do you know if you have the ability to perform?...*especially* at the highest levels possible? You begin to work—on yourself...on your dream...on that thing you want to master or be known for. And you don't stop at the first instance of negative feedback—from yourself or others. This is where most people screw up. They stop working to uncover and improve on an ability that is hidden in their DNA, waiting to be groomed. They fall into the mindset of "This is how it's always going to be" or "Those genes don't run in my family."

It's the same type of person who takes a personality assessment and believes what the thirty-page, auto-generated report says is final...that there's no room for change.

What happens is they miss out on factors like these:

- All the feedback that comes with failing during the journey

- Lessons in humility

- Learning to ask for help

- Clarity surrounding what skills and talents they are passionate about and can master

- Overcoming adversity

All because, at first blush, they didn't appear to have the ability. Then, later, they lament, "This *could* have been me." I remember as a young high-school athlete, I was told I didn't have the *ability* to play college baseball at the highest levels. These naysayers were basing their opinions on my *current* ability, not on my *future* capacity to perform. So I sought out coaches, drills, mentors, examples…everything I could get my hands on to uncover the truth about my ability to play college baseball.

After eighteen months of blisters, self-doubt, trial, error, and getting beat by my peers, I got the feedback I needed. I had the ability. It was just a matter of continuing to search for those habits and strategies that would work, *for me*, in grooming that ability. You must understand—what works for others doesn't necessarily work for you.

You must find what works for you. Shortcuts don't exist when it comes to your best performance. And if my story doesn't convince you, just ask Michael Jordan, one of the greatest basketball players to have ever played the game. He had to first uncover that he had athletic *ability* to play basketball… because many told him he didn't.

To do so, Michael had to identify the habits and strategies that worked for him—the ones necessary to perform at his highest levels. Then he had to commit to them…every day. And when he stepped onto the court to attempt his best possible performance, he had to "carry into effect, fulfill, discharge" all those habits and strategies he so diligently worked to own.

He realized performance started *within*. Again, no magic pill. No cookie-cutter tactic. And now he's part of history. In fact, he's a legend in sports—his legacy lives on. Did you catch that? Legacy is the by-product of consistent, high-level performance. Do you want to leave a legacy? In the marketplace? In sports? At *home*? I know you do.

So let's uncover *your* abilities—the ones necessary for you to perform at your highest levels and leave your legacy with four P's. Let's call this the Four-Step Plan to Your Greatest Performances (yes, plural!):

1. **Prepare.** Identify what you want to master, and then determine what you believe will help you uncover your unique ability to perform in that area. Feel free to study what habits and tools others used to help them, *but be willing to adapt them to fit yourself.*

2. **Play.** You have to put your preparation to the test. Take what you've worked on, and then get in the game! Take a leap of faith, for cryin' out loud!

3. **Persist.** You're bound to fail. But the highest-performing people in this world keep pushing through the failure because they know there is wisdom in it...wisdom that will help them readjust, reassess, and redo. Keep pushing. It's for your own good.

4. **Permit.** The performance journey is marked by reinvention, revolution, and resolution. Underperformers look for others' permission to do something. On the other hand, high performers *give themselves permission* to improve on their current state, go against the grain, and figure out why failure occurred.

Performance is not a one-time event leading to a specific outcome. It's a journey leading to generations of impact.

Don't rely on the pill or quick fix. Create your own magic, Baby!

> *"Some people want it to happen, some wish it would happen, others make it happen."*
>
> **—Michael Jordan**

Performance is written by James Reid (J. R.)

"I think sales is the most important skill set young people can learn. Understanding how to pitch an idea with confidence and secure a client are valuable skills that apply to every single aspect of business."

—Jennifer Hyman

/piCH/

Noun

1. *The quality of a sound governed by the rate of vibrations producing it; the degree of highness or lowness of a tone*

2. *The steepness of a slope, especially of a roof*

Verb

1. *(Baseball) Throw (the ball) for the batter to try to hit; throw or fling roughly or casually*

2. *A form of words used when trying to persuade someone to buy or accept something*

3. *A swaying or oscillation of a ship, aircraft, or vehicle around a horizontal axis perpendicular to the direction of motion*

Even though I grew up in a very small town of one thousand people, because it was in Texas, it forced me to want to do everything *big*! As a young man, I was always intrigued by someone who could motivate people to want to do something, or go somewhere, or even more impressive, spend their hard-earned money!

I remember hearing the words and watching the faces of the people set in a trance by a man outside the circus tent in my town of Dumas. He created such a desire that I just had to see what he was talking about.

I heard a quote by the Greatest Showman...the infamous P. T. Barnum, He stated that "Without promotion, something terrible happens... nothing!" So that was it...I decided then that I was going to help people get what they needed, even if they did not realize it at the current moment. I decided to help people go where they needed to go, do what they needed to do, and even buy what they needed to buy. That is ultimately how business works. But it all starts with the pitch.

I find it so interesting that the word *pitch* has so many meanings yet always produces something greater. The word *pitch* can be a perfect tone, a well-thrown ball, or a good flow of water from a roof.

However, for this illustration, I will move into the inner working of the word *pitch* in reference to a sales exchange. During a sales exchange, the pitch itself is very often met with resistance energy, which creates a negative vibration that usually brings the sales exchange to an automatic "No" or "Not interested. Send me an email, and I'll look at it." Getting to *yes* takes perfection in timing.

Calling the pitch a "sales presentation" is part of the perception surrounding the sales process. So how can someone be uncomfortable with the pitch and still be motivated to buy? I have included here some of the skills I have developed over many years of selling or pitching my wares.

In the game of baseball, a good pitcher strives to strike the batter out. The batter, on the other hand, strives to make perfect contact combined with perfect timing to knock the ball out of the park. But in sales, a perfected "pitch" is one that connects all the moving parts and gets your message out to the world in perfect harmony. Sales is helping people solve a problem with a service or a product. The greater the problem solved, the greater the price people are willing to pay.

As a standalone "pitch," however, effective selling is something of a well-tuned form of precision movement between people. Get your story straight, and learn how to tell your story for maximum effect. Understand how your VIM—Vision–Innovation–Motivation—will mesh with their business and enhance it. It's your story, and how you choose to deliver it is up to you. A well-tuned story will make you relatable, and when people can relate to you, you have what it takes to be successful.

Along with the science of sales is a bit of magic. The types of information most likely to convince a person to buy, or help them understand what you're talking about, can be broken down to an elementary level, so don't make it too complicated.

The "pitch" is where a large part of this sales presentation gets done. If you have a product or a service, you should be able to pitch it to an interested person in a one-, a three-, and even a five-minute version. The challenge often is that we know what we know…and it is usually *way* too much information about what we do or about the product we are trying to get someone to purchase.

To me, PITCH stands for *Perfection in Timing Creates Harmony*. That is my acronym for *pitch*. The right thing at the wrong time does not end up well…or so I discovered when I asked my girlfriend to marry me. OK, we were six years old. Some people just seem to know what to say and when. I believe that timing is a keen sense to go, slow down, or stop. The good news is, I believe it can be taught. How? By watching a master do it and then letting him or her watch you try. Be ready for some critical comments. After all, you want to win, right?

Here are the five steps to mastering your pitch:

P – Prepare with creating your story. (The best presentations are two-thirds stories, not just facts!)

I – Involve the experts to watch and share their observations.

T – Try, and try again.

C – Challenge yourself to listen to the comments, even when they hurt.

H – Help others after you master your pitch.

What is your pitch?...Let's get ready for something *big*!

> *"Every day, you got to do adjustments. Every pitch. You gotta do what it takes."*
>
> **—Miguel Cabrera**

Pitch is written by Michael Bray

"Relax, recharge, and reflect. Sometimes it's OK to do nothing."

—Izey Victoria Odiase

Recharge

re·charge

/rēˈCHärj/

Verb

1. Restore an electric charge to (a battery or a battery-operated device) by connecting it to a device that draws power from another source of electricity

Noun

1. The replenishment of an aquifer by the absorption of water

I'm a farm boy—or at least I grew up on a tobacco farm. I really wasn't good at farming. Too much waiting on things I had no control over. On a farm, you have less control than you may think. So I went to college and started my career.

Nothing new except I kept missing the farm—or that's what I thought. It has been more than forty years since I lived on the farm. What I missed was the pace of life, but I didn't understand that.

Everything is about seasons. You can't put in extra hours of work and cause things to grow. You have to plant seeds in fields, water and fertilize them, and then wait for them to germinate. And wait and wait…for something to happen. I don't like waiting. I'm not very good at it. In fact, I really suck at waiting. I don't like lines, haircuts, dental appointments, going to the bank, or airlines. Just not wired to wait.

But waiting is an important part of productivity. Some years, there were fields we would not use for growing because the soil needed to rest. When I was young, I didn't understand why, so I asked my dad. He said that letting the fields rest made them recharge and become more powerful for plant growth.

Since learning that, I realized that we have an inner world that controls our outer world. Thanks to Dr. Maxwell Maltz's epic book, *Psycho-Cybernetics*, I have begun to appreciate the need to rest and *recharge*. I once read an article on author Malcolm Gladwell's famous "10,000-hour-rule." You may have heard the part about it how it takes thousands of hours to perfect a skill like writing, music, or even golf. Well, maybe not golf. I don't think Tiger Woods would say he has perfected that frustrating game. The golf course is the only place in the world where prayer does not work.

Anyway, the young, brilliant students mentioned in the 10,000-hour study did something many don't know about. Once they had spent six hours or so every day perfecting their skills, they would rest. Yep. Do nothing—but rest or play. Apparently, goofing off was as important as putting calluses on your fingers practicing the violin for endless hours straight.

Another article I read said that most heart attacks in America occur around nine o'clock in the morning. Must be the morning rush hour in Los Angeles. The article went on to say that there is a small group of people in America who rarely have heart attacks—our Jewish friends. It seems, in their culture, they are taught to not only rise early but to ease into their day. They do this every morning by swinging by the synagogue to pray, sing a few songs, and chat with their friends. By the time they hit the office to conquer the day, they've had a recharging of sorts.

I'm not Jewish, but I do practice something similar and have learned to steal a little from my early farm life. Like my Jewish friends, I wake up pretty early, at around 5 a.m., go to my lanai (that's a back porch in Florida), and talk to God as I understand Him. I listen to a little music and read something positive that I'm interested in, and then I head to the shower. So far, it has worked for me. I'm still around after fifty-eight years—and no heart attacks, thank God.

I'm not sure how insane your work schedule is, but I work six days a week and do nothing on Mondays except goof off. This way, I remind myself that recharging is as important as working...and even God took a day off!

If we learn to step back, slow down, unplug it, and recharge, it might be the most important activity to our success. Lance Whitt, in his amazing book *Replenish*, says there are four R's involved in recharging:

1. **Rest** (sabbatical). We know we should...we just generally don't.

2. **Reflection** (retreat). Get away. Find your "happy place."

3. **Recreation** (vacation). Take one, and *really* unplug...I dare ya.

4. **Renewal** (starting afresh). Cultivate new thoughts and pure ideas.

If we don't practice proper recharging, then we may find ourselves burning out. I've done that in the past, and that's as bad as a root canal. No doubt we can resort to our default setting and pay the price if we don't do something different. That usually does not end well. So stop...plug into what charges you, rinse, and repeat. Then, maybe, you can actually *recharge* at something...you know—to charge at something again.

> *"One of the best ways to recharge is by simply being in the presence of art. No thoughts, no critiques. Just full-on absorption mode."*
>
> **—Dean Francis Alfar**

Recharge is written by Alex Anderson

"From now on, I want you to practice reframing other people's negativity as a reminder of how not to be."

—T. Harv Eker

/rē ˈfrām/

Verb

1. *Place (a picture or photograph) in a new frame*

2. *Frame or express (words or a concept or plan) differently; overcoming life's obstacles*

What happens when life fails to produce the outcome you anticipated? What happens when everything you've worked for disappears?

In 2009, I found myself in one of the biggest setbacks I'd ever faced, like many other Americans during the economic crisis. I thought my life was coming to an end. I couldn't believe it…I'd lost everything. Everything! My job, my career, my marriage, and myself. My life as I knew it was over.

So what do you do when everything around you crumbles? My solution?

Reframe!

Well, it's easier said than done, but the brave one who steps up for the challenge will soon see that relationships improve, quality of life increases, and contentment becomes a close friend.

Have you ever found yourself imprisoned by a thought, an image, a fantasy, a dream, a career, or even a relationship? Maybe you are boxed into a religious cycle or a family ideology. Whatever it is that is keeping you from pursuing your dream attaining maximum success in your life...I want to encourage you to reframe your negative thoughts, and *let go*!

Letting go of the drama in your world might not be that easy. You've probably heard the saying, "Life's a stage, and everybody's playing a part." What's unfortunate about this statement is that those trapped in the dramatic roles of the victim, the underdog, the codependent partner, or the abandoned child forfeit the opportunity to become the superstar (lead role) of their lives. Why? Because these are supporting roles, and until you begin to reframe your life, you will never claim your dreams and successes.

The ability to reframe is just as much about knowing *when* to let go as it is about knowing *how* to let go. As a cognitive behavioral therapist, I use *thought restructuring or modification* as a key fundamental techniques with clients. In layman's terms, this simply means changing how you think. This sounds very much like a cliché; however, you will never change your life without changing how you think about your life.

So, what does it mean to reframe? Let's begin with the prefix: *re*. According to various dictionary definitions, *re* means "again, anew, recall, back to the original place, condition, etc." The word *frame* means "to conceive or imagine, as an idea." When combined into one word, *re* and *frame* mean "to look at, present, or think of (beliefs, ideas, relationships, etc.) in a new or different way."

This simple definition can encompass the difference (or the gap) between a life filled with joy or depression, between anxiety and contentment, or between addiction and self-control. To reframe is a simple concept, but it is a challenge to apply it to our everyday lives.

In my practice, my goal is often to encourage clients to identify faulty thought processes and maladaptive schemas that produce negative emotions and unwanted behaviors. Cognitive Behavioral Therapy (CBT) is used to address a variety of problems and is the therapeutic approach for many counselors due to its immediate results. Once the presenting problem is identified and isolated, CBT can quickly help clients reduce symptoms by developing coping skills, managing their anger and emotions, making adjustments, and treating grief and trauma.

CBT also treats mental health conditions including depression, anxiety, sexual disorders, personality disorders, and eating disorders. By addressing negative automatic thoughts and maladaptive schemas, the client develops coping skills and behavior changes to minimize distress. So, in layman's terms, if you can reframe your thoughts, you can reframe your life and embrace your success!

Ten years after the economic crisis, I used these seven steps to reframe that devastating experience. Notice that the first letters in the strategies below form the word "reframe":

R – **Review your past successes and failures.** Reviewing our strengths and areas of growth allows us to leverage our experiences for greater success.

E – **Evaluate past strategies used.** Determine what works and what does not. Adopt new life strategies to pursue greater successes.

F – **Focus on the positive.** Be grateful for what you have and for the potential to grow.

R – **Restructure negative thoughts.** Embrace the simplicity of changing a negative thought into a positive thought.

A – **Activate your new strategy for success.** Once you have your new strategy, enlist a support team to help you execute it.

M – **Maintain your new strategy using a maintenance plan.** Once you have executed your strategy, find effective ways to maintain positive growth.

E – **Enjoy and engage in a meaningful life, on purpose.** Be intentional, and live life without apologies.

The art of reframing begins by shifting a negative to a positive; the art of reframing ends when you embrace a more positive perspective for a happier, fulfilled life.

"Instead of saying, 'I'm damaged, I'm broken, I have trust issues,' say, 'I'm healing, I'm rediscovering myself, I'm starting over.'"

—Horacio Jones

Reframe is written by Dr. Jada Jackson

"When you fail at something, the best thing to do is think back to your successes, and try to replicate whatever you did to make them happen."

—Rosabeth Moss Kanter

/ˈreplə͵kāt/

Verb

1. *Make an exact copy of; reproduce*

Noun

/ˈreplikət/

1. *Of the nature of a copy*

2. *A close or exact copy; a replica*

3. *(Music) A tone one or more octaves above or below the given tone*

In all my life, I have not been able to find a more powerful word than *replicate*—except maybe the word *grace*.

The ability to *replicate* can be a blessing or a curse in your business and personal life. Much of life is how you cast it—what light you cast your victories and defeats in, whom you cast as the key actors in the play we call life, and where you cast your worries and concerns when they become too much to bear. These actions we commit every day can be our rule or our ruin, and we do these things to ourselves over and over again. We replicate them.

Replication is the act of reproducing a result. You can't have a result without participation. Life either happens to you, or you hurl your will upon it. Actively or passively, life continues to happen, and we all have a role in it. When good things happen to us, we rarely ask, "Why is this happening to me?" But when life goes poorly, we lament, thrusting our hands toward the sky, exclaiming, "Why is this happening to me?" and sometimes "Why does this *always* happen to me?"

Maybe you just don't understand the concept of replication. Maybe you created a system of replication and built a machine that produces the same results over and over in your life.

Results are what we all want. Give me results. I love the results! Results can be measured. Results can be quantified. I can be praised for my results. Results might even gain me favor with my most important relationships. I judge my performance by my results. After all, is not a tree judged by its fruit—a *result*?

However, if your life has not gone well and your machine is running funky, the results might be addiction, divorce, debt, unemployment, underemployment, spiritual darkness, hate, fear, loneliness, apathy, and poor self-esteem. You might self-describe as a loser because you're not winning.

To replicate is a to have a "more" concept. If you want more of what you have, you replicate the things that you want more of. If you want more sales, you do more advertising, right? *No—absolutely not!* As a technique for replicating, whatever you mean by *more* needs to be qualified. You want more of the good stuff, not the bad stuff, right? Some of your advertising might be drawing the wrong customers and driving your overall average sale down.

You need the right customers, so you need more of the advertising that gets you the right customers, and you need to prune away the advertising that brings in the wrong customers. You must identify the *more* you actually need.

A lot of work goes on before and after the concept of replication. We want more of the good things in our lives. Replicating the same old junk over and over while expecting a different result is the basic definition of insanity. The best way to avoid this is to take an inventory of all the things you think are going well in your life. Good things are happening, *believe me*—you just need to recognize them.

Here is a simple five-step system I use every day to win way more often than I lose, accomplishing seemingly impossible tasks on a regular basis:

1. **Be deliberate**. Have a written plan. Goals are plans!

2. **Execute**. Get off the couch, and work your plan. This is the hardest step, by far.

3. **Analyze**. Stop, reflect, and measure your results. Prune away the bad, and focus on the good.

4. **Replicate**. Do more of the good stuff, and drop the bad stuff. It's that simple.

5. **Systemize**. Once you have identified the good stuff that can be replicated to create a system, it perpetuates.

Understand that this is not easy. Nothing admirable is ever easily accomplished, and success rarely goes uncriticized. You will know you are truly getting traction in making your life better when Satan attacks you through your family, friends, circumstances, and life. When that happens, relish it. You are now significant! Satan only attacks those he is worried about losing.

The late Zig Ziglar said, "We are all designed for accomplishment, engineered for success, endowed by the Creator with the seeds of greatness." God wants you to live a powerful life, but you may have to make some changes. The concept of replication might mean pruning away some negative results and influences before entering the replication stage. This is a hard teaching. However, once you do you that, you can take ownership of your life and start replicating good fruits and success in your wheel of life—spiritually, personally, and professionally.

"We are all designed for accomplishment, engineered for success, endowed by the Creator with the seeds of greatness."
—Zig Ziglar

Replicate is written by AC Lockyer

"Be aware of what season you are in, and give yourself the grace to be there."

—Kristen Dalton

Season

sea·son

/ˈsēzən/

Noun

1. *Each of the four divisions of the year (spring, summer, autumn, and winter) marked by particular weather patterns and daylight hours, resulting from the earth's changing position with regard to the sun*

2. *A set or sequence of related television programs*

Verb

1. *Add salt, herbs, pepper, or other spices to (food)*

Growing up in Wisconsin allowed me to experience the four *seasons*—sometimes in the extreme.

I loved summer as a kid, swimming, playing outside...it was so awesome! (We did not have video games back then.) Then the leaves started to change colors, and a fresh coolness became a new reality, autumn was awesome.

I remember taking hikes in northern Wisconsin, and even as a child, I enjoyed all the amazing colors! But then winter came howling in...but I loved the snow. Sledding, snowmobiling, and tubing—that was a total blast. But then when it started to warm up and the tulips would begin to bloom...the smells...wow...that was awesome! I love springtime.

That was many years ago. Now I live in Texas, and it seems that there are only two seasons: summer and not as summer. To be honest, I actually miss the seasons. I enjoyed the variety.

But in my life, that does not seem to be the case...at least at first glance. I mean, we have times in our lives when it seems nothing is growing. Other times, everything is blooming, and the birds seem to be singing more than normal. I actually fought with myself the other day, wishing that every day would be the same. But then I thought, "Wait...that would be horrible. Too predictable." I suddenly realized that it could actually be *boring* if every day were the same!

You see, I love the variety. So why would I even consider wanting my life to be monotonous? The variety of life is where it is at. Seasons are awesome! It is interesting that the first definition of "season" as a noun pertains to seasons. They start and end—just like the seasons in our lives.

The definition of "season" as a verb concerns accenting food using "seasoning." I was at a friend's home the other day, and he had some almonds in the pantry. I *love* almonds! I was excited to get this well-deserved snack, so I took a big handful. *Yuck!* It was like eating sawdust! I made a face like I had just sucked on a lemon and said, "What's wrong with these? They are horrible!"

My friend said. "Oh, they are unsalted."

They were bland. They needed some *seasoning*.

That brings us to the subject of life. Do you want a bland, eventless life? No? Me neither. The reality is, most of us do like variety. We love the ups and downs, like in the seasons. When the views change, it makes each day an adventure. I wonder why I seem to resist change so much, especially in my own life, and especially as I get older. I *need* change on a regular basis. It makes life interesting. It seasons it and makes it more…"tasty."

Here are five tips for embracing the seasons of life:

1. Do not resist the seasons; you cannot stop them from coming.

2. Understand that the seasons of life bring ups and downs, and that keeps things interesting.

3. Recognize that the seasons bring tasty adventures.

4. Realize that if you do not like the season you are in, just wait…it *will* change.

5. Help others navigate their seasons.

"To everything there is a season, and a time to every purpose under heaven."

—Ecclesiastes 3:1 (BSB), by King Solomon, the wisest person of all time

Season is written by Dr. Sam Farina

"To shine your brightest light is to be who you truly are."

—Roy T. Bennett

/SHīn/

Verb

1. *(Of the sun or another source of light) Give out a bright light*

2. *Be very talented or perform very well*

Noun

1. *A quality of brightness, especially from reflected light*

You may have seen my magic on prime-time TV or late-night talk shows, or maybe you are among the billions who have viewed my magic online. But my career did not start there. I grew up in a magical family with magicians as parents. I don't remember most of my childhood because most of it was spent in a magic trunk or dark box. That's not child abuse, that's just magic!

I grew up in Minnesota. My dad said, "The Midwest is the land of opportunity…if you're a tractor." So I knew I needed to get out and develop my show to *shine*. After graduating from high school, I moved to the small showbiz town of Branson, Missouri, spent more money than my family had, and built a grand magic show. I was going to shine *big* time!

I had a theater. I had billboards. All the best Vegas magic props. Dancing girls. Cool lights, and even a sparkly leather jacket…talk about *shine*! I planned according to the famous line in the movie *Field of Dreams*: "Build it, and they will come…"

Well…they didn't.

It was a painful lesson to grasp, and did I mention expensive? Branson was home to more than 150 shows, all competing for the same audience. I learned that just getting a bunch of expensive props, hiring some dancing girls, having cool lights, and having a place to perform in a tourist town was *not* enough! To stand out, one needs to *shine*. That painful reality set me on a journey to figure out how to do just that. I wanted to shine, but not just so people could just see me. I wanted to reflect a brighter light. To be honest, for me, that light has been the Light I get from my faith. That meant letting God's light shine though me by doing what He created me to do.

When I set out to discover the real me, it changed everything. Discovering my *shine* put me on televisions and the largest stages in America and in front of one *billion* viewers on social media…yes, I said, one billion with a "b."

Magicians usually don't share our secrets…but here is my secret formula I now use for myself and countless others to discover how to really shine:

S – **Soul**: The innermost part of who you really are. It is your mind and emotions. It is your will…*why* you do what you do.

H – **Heart**: The thing that excites you and brings your passion out. It makes your heart beat faster. It gives you life. It is something you love to do.

I – **Individual personality**: Each of us is a unique, special individual. Be *you*!

N – **Natural ability**: The thing you are good at doing. Each of us has something we're better at than most. It's God's special gifting.

E – **Experience**: Life experience, that which brings wisdom. Your past experiences guide your future.

There is no shortcut to being able to shine. It takes time. It takes courage. I challenge you to dig in. Discover *you*. Find out what excites you. Be you, not a copy of someone else. See what you are better than average at doing. And after doing that for a while, you will *shine*...I promise!

"You are on a soulful path that asks you to step into the greatest version of yourself. It is a sacred gift to shine your brightest light—not just in your moments of glory, but each day."

—Debbie Ford

Shine is written by Justin Flom

> *"Peace is a journey of a thousand miles, and it*
> *must be taken one step at a time."*
>
> **—Lyndon B. Johnson**

/step/

Noun

1. *An act or movement of putting one leg in front of the other in walking or running*

2. *A flat surface, especially one in a series, on which to place one's foot when moving from one level to another*

Verb

1. *Lift and set down one's foot or one foot after the other in order to walk somewhere or move to a new position*

2. *(Nautical) Set up (a mast) in its step*

Most likely, we don't know each other, but I'll dare to guess we have at least one thing in common: who we are today is not who we want to be tomorrow.

You wouldn't have picked up this book if it weren't true. There is still so much I want to achieve in this life. I want to be a better person. I want to leave a bigger legacy. I want to build something great. I want my life to have impact beyond what it would if today were my last day.

As big as my dreams may be, my doubts are often bigger. Does my past define my future? Am I too old? Am I too young? Do I really have what it takes?

My hunch is, you've probably been plagued by questions like these. Questions are good, but sometimes we don't even bother to ask them—we jump straight to telling ourselves, "I'm too old, I'm too young, I'm not smart enough. I could never do that."

If we do this long enough, we lose all hope to dream. We don't dare to reach for something bigger, for fear that we'll just be disappointed. The moment a hopeful thought seeps up, we slam it back down. We might even pat ourselves on the back for not allowing that annoying little dream to ruin our day. "Take that, nagging feeling! I'll teach you not to interrupt my comfortable life." The worst part is, we usually don't even realize we're doing this.

We've become distracted by the "proverbial mile" that stands between us and our goals. It's sometimes our biggest opponent because the enormity of the work needed to achieve our dreams is crippling. And that's the problem: we see everything we need to accomplish instead of looking for the one thing we *can* accomplish—the *step*.

When we focus on the mile, we lose sight of the *step*. When we lose sight of the step, we don't move. And when we don't move, our dreams, our desires, and potentially our destiny go unfulfilled.

It's a natural part of what we do. In fact, we must look at the mile. It's typically the first thing we do when trying to size up our ability to achieve a goal. If we never looked at the mile, we would never know what it takes to get where we want to go. The problem is not in looking at the mile but in getting *stuck* focusing on the mile. Our brains are constantly trying to evaluate where we are in relation to the mile and what's still left to accomplish our goals. Too often, the mile can feel overwhelming. That's why we need to train ourselves to think and act differently, focusing on one step at a time.

The mile (aka our ferocious enemy) is not as big and bad as he may seem.

But don't take him for granted. He'll jump up and have you stuck before you realize what's happening. In fact, his job is to trick us into believing we can't accomplish the thing we desire, therefore rendering us stagnant. He's a liar.

My wife and I were watching one of our favorite shows, *NCIS*, and one of the main characters, Ducky, made this statement: "When you are overwhelmed, do something you know you can accomplish, and suddenly you won't be quite so overwhelmed."

I love this statement. It sums up a lot of what the word *step* means to me. It's a powerful principle, yet so simple to understand. Typically, in those moments of being paralyzed by the overwhelming number of tasks we believe it will take to accomplish our goals, we simply can't move, or we can't decide how to move.

We can't move because we're looking at the wrong thing. We're looking at *everything* we need to accomplish instead of looking at the *one thing* we can accomplish.

The great news is that the biggest setbacks can be overcome by shifting your focus back to the smallest step. This kind of refocusing is not a one-time occurrence. The mile will tempt you again and again, and that's OK. When you're overwhelmed, stop and think about one small thing you can do now. Then make that your only goal.

My simple advice is to find your step, take it, and then take the next, and the next so that five or ten years down road, you don't look back with regret about what you could have accomplished, but instead look back with satisfaction about what you have accomplished.

> *"The man who removes a mountain begins by carrying away small stones."*
> **—Chinese Proverb**

Step is written by Chris Capehart

"The universe is made of stories, not of atoms."

—Muriel Rukeyser

Story

sto·ry

/ˈstôrē/

Noun

1. *An account of imaginary or real people and events told for entertainment*
2. *An account of past events in someone's life or in the evolution of something*

We humans are fascinated with stories. Oh, the genre doesn't matter. It could be a romantic comedy, a sci-fi thriller, or an action adventure. We just like a good *story*. When you go to the office on Monday morning, what do you want to hear? A good story that someone had from their weekend. What is a great way to open a meeting, a presentation, or even a Sunday-morning sermon? A good story.

What is it that fascinates us with the power of story? I think perhaps it's the awareness that each of us is in the midst of living out our own life story. Maybe you are living out a real page-turner. Or maybe your life right now seems like it could be bottled and sold as a sleep aid. Either way, you have an awareness that your own life is a living, unfolding story filled with some level of intrigue, mystery, and adventure. And the best part of your own story is that the ending is not yet written. Or, depending on your philosophy of life, even if it's already been written, it hasn't been revealed to you.

So how can you harness the power of story, our human fascination with story, to be a better leader?

Find the story behind your business. Simon Sinek wrote a bestselling book titled *Start with Why*. In it, he shares the principle that truly inspired communicators don't just *tell* their audience or their prospective customers what they do, or how they do it; they share with them the *why* behind the product or service they offer. The *why* speaks to their beliefs, their values, and their motivation for doing what they do.

Consumers find this compelling in part because sharing these details often involves telling your organizational story. People want to do business with people they know and trust. Let your audience get to know you by telling them *why* you do what you do, not just *how* you do it better than the competition. That telling involves sharing your story.

Maybe you are a chiropractor who is board-certified, highly skilled, and offers great results at a fair price. Awesome…but chances are, so do fifty other chiropractors within a twenty-mile radius of where you practice. But none of your competitors has your story—the reasons why you got into helping people get well through chiropractic medicine. Tell them!

Mine the stories from your business. My wife wanted to buy a digital picture frame. She went online and looked up several options. Did she read the specs on screen brightness and memory storage? Nope. What she read were the reviews. You see, what mattered to my wife was what other people who purchased the product had to say, what their experience was. What was their story?

Your customers' testimonials, their reviews, are their stories, their adventures, and their experiences with you, your product, or your service. So be intentional in asking for, highlighting, and celebrating the success stories from your business.

There are five core elements of every story: plot, character, setting, theme, and conflict. How can you share these with the people you most want to attract and influence? Let's look at these five core elements in the context of your business's story:

- **Plot**. Where is your business going? What are your goals? If your company were a train, what would make both employees and customers want to get on board?

- **Character**. Who are the main players in your company story? Do you allow your audience to get to know them? Are they likable?

- **Setting**. Are you operating in an expanding market, a crowded market, a changing market? A well-known or niche market?

- **Theme**. What does your organization stand for? What are your values?

- **Conflict**. When something goes wrong, how do you handle it? You can't please everyone 100 percent of the time. When you shipped something late or to the wrong address, how did you handle it? Rather than pretending things never go wrong, how can you show and celebrate how you resolve customer conflict? Let's be honest—all stories, even Hallmark movies, have some form of conflict embedded into the plot. Without it, a story is, frankly, boring.

May you live a life and run an organization today that makes for a great story—one that generations to come will be telling!

> *"Storytelling is the most powerful way to put*
> *ideas into the world today."*
>
> **—Robert McKee**

Story is written by David W. Welday III

"Few people attain great lives, in large part because it is just so easy to settle for a good life."

—Jim Collins

Tenacity

te·nac·i·ty

/təˈnasədē/

Noun

1. *The quality or fact of being able to grip something firmly; grip*

2. *The quality or fact of continuing to exist; persistence*

Tenacity. In our everyday lives, we often view *tenacity* as an intangible ability to rise above obstacles, despite circumstances. Related words include *grit, endurance, perseverance,* and *relentless determination.*

However, there are some subtle differences between the word *tenacity* and its related counterparts. Although all imply some form of persistence, the word *tenacity* also implies *strategic* thinking. A tenacious person works smarter, not necessarily harder, than a persistent person. He or she is in it for the long haul and will do what is strategically required to accomplish a goal.

Where does tenacious ability come from? How does one come to possess it? Is tenacity an innate ability or a learned behavior?

Some people are tenacious spirits as a result of dire circumstances. However, that does not mean that all people who encounter dire circumstances are tenacious. Those who do possess tenacity are often viewed as an anomaly of sorts. Their inspiring stories about overcoming oppression, homelessness, poverty, poor health, and many other types of adversity are often the topic of biographies and noteworthy recognition. Many effective motivational speakers draw on their past challenging experiences to inspire others to do the same. Their relentless pursuit to overcome adversity or attain a goal is noteworthy and worth examining.

Do they possess a special "X" factor that the general population doesn't? As a professor in the field of gifted education, I have spent many years studying gifted and high-ability individuals, traits of giftedness, and high-ability and high-potential students in all socio-economic settings. Many would think that those being born super smart would naturally become super successful and be fantastic leaders. However, this is simply not the case.

Those who are tenacious can continuously outperform many (if not most) academically gifted individuals who do not possess tenacity. Tenacious individuals are found in every socio-economic class, and their cunning and resourceful behaviors are easily recognizable when encountering them one-on-one. You will find them among the poorest of neighborhoods or in the workplace as thought leaders and innovators. We admire their strength and sheer determination that led to overcoming what we perceive to be insurmountable obstacles and/or achieving their goals. Whether intentional or not, they often inspire us to find our own inner strength and courage that provoke greatness. They possess resolve to face what many of us would fear. Their approach to problem solving defies standard logic and reasoning. For reference, think Chris Gardner, the homeless salesman portrayed by Will Smith in the biographical film *The Pursuit of Happyness* (2006, Sony Pictures).

Great, tenacious leaders are goal setters, goal seekers, and accomplishers. Their commitment to a cause allows them to treat obstacles as an opportunity for growth. They possess "a growth mindset as opposed to a fixed mindset," a phrase coined by renowned psychologist Dr. Carol Dweck. Dweck spent decades studying people's mindset toward failure. She noticed that some individuals rebounded after encountering failure, while others were devastated after experiencing the smallest setback. Her research uncovered a link between mindset and achievement.

Simultaneously, the field of neuroscience revealed the malleable "plasticity" of the brain—that is, the brain's ability to change with experience. The implications of these discoveries are twofold.

First, we now know we can actually increase our neural growth by the type of deliberate actions we take. Yes, action! If you think of this in terms of the *nature* (genetic inheritance/biological factors) vs. *nurture* (environment/learning experiences) debate, what we now know is that we can most assuredly *nurture* certain behaviors through conditioning. We can actually increase our IQ, competencies, skills, and knowledge through action!

Second, we now know we are able to move from a fixed mindset to a growth mindset. This means that if you don't currently possess a particular disposition, you can if pursue a growth mindset. Simply put, your approach matters. For example, two very goal-oriented people might tackle the same problem. Both people work very hard trying to achieve their goal. However, one applies the same method over and over, even when it is flawed. His productivity declines, despite his work ethic. Over time, he might become discouraged and give up altogether. Although his efforts are valiant, he never achieves his goal.

The other person implements the method once, analyzes the results, and implements positive change, learning from each iteration of implementation. Furthermore, his early failures are not a setback. He believes he can achieve his intended outcome. In other words, failure is not an option. He achieves his goal.

You can achieve your goals, too. Here are five G's to help you develop tenacious behaviors:

1. **Goals.** Set clear goals that are broken down into achievable baby steps. Approach it like weight loss. You might want to lose twenty pounds, but it is easier to (mentally) chip away at the goal when you set it in five-pound increments.

2. **Guidance.** Look continuously to your surroundings, including unlikely people, resources, and mentors, for guidance. Every person is an expert at something. Analyze what you have learned, and implement change to hone your strategy.

3. **Growth.** Embrace a growth mindset. Be comfortable with being uncomfortable. You will experience the greatest growth mindset when you are uncomfortable. You will eventually learn to live and conduct business fearlessly.

4. **Gurus.** Look up, not sideways! Surround yourself with goal seekers and reachers...the thought-provoking gurus of your industry.

5. **Grit.** Get gritty. Thick-skinned, gritty people do not allow setbacks to discourage them. They will persevere, despite their circumstances and naysayers.

I will close by encouraging you to take care of yourself spiritually, mentally, and physically while pursuing lofty goals. If it were easy, everyone would be doing it. There is a reason why "one is the loneliest number."

The word *tenacity* reminds me of a slogan found on my favorite coffee mug. It simply states, "She believed she could, so she did"—an example of a *growth* mindset approach to achieving a goal. The *fixed* mindset version of this slogan might be, "Others couldn't, so she didn't." Both statements illustrate the effects of surrounding yourself with like-minded people. To quote Confucius, "If you are the smartest person in the room, then you are in the wrong room."

"You may encounter many defeats, but you must not be defeated. In fact, it may be necessary to encounter the defeats, so you can know who you are, what you can rise from, how you can still come out of it."

—**Maya Angelou**

Tenacity is written by Dr. Alicia Cotabish

"I think, therefore, I am."

—René Descartes

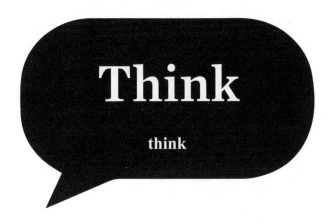

/THiNGk/

Verb

1. *Have a particular opinion, belief, or idea about someone or something*

2. *Direct one's mind toward someone or something; use one's mind actively to form connected ideas*

Noun, informal

1. *An act of thinking*

It is impossible to even consider the word *think* without, as a prerequisite, actually *doing* this word. As proposed in the quote by Descartes, the most fundamental activity of being human is to think. He would even say that "thinking" establishes the fact of our existence. I would say it also creates the *quality* of our existence.

Our superpower as humans is not simply that we think. Thinking can be as unconscious as the act of breathing: "There is a stoplight. Oh, look, a cat! I am hungry…" Our minds operate without our intentional direction.

Our superpower, then, is that we can actually think about thinking. And if we can think about thinking, then we can also think about thinking about thinking. We can get above our own thoughts, and above the thoughts we have about our thoughts. The reason this a superpower is because when (and only when) we do this, we can direct the course of our own lives and potentially even the lives of others.

The human mind is incredibly powerful, yet limited to whatever barriers lie within its own current thought process. The kind of thinking that transforms destinies and cultures first begins with thinking differently.

Let me be clear: thinking *differently* is not the same as thinking *different*. Thinking differently is a shift in thought *process*, while thinking different is merely a change in thought *content*.

Thought content is that which comes into your mind, while *thought process* is what your mind does with it. *Optimism* is a thought process that can make bad news good, while *pessimism* is a thought process that can make good news bad. Change a thought process, and everything else in your mind changes.

Therefore, our capacity to think about thinking is a superpower. Those who will not make the effort to do so will always remain stuck within self-imposed but unrecognized limitations. Those who think about their thinking will unlock the vast potential of the human mind.

I sat with a client once who wanted strategies to help with his anger. He was the last client I met with on certain days, and every time I saw him, I was on the last fumes of my own emotional tank. So, contrary to the rules of good therapy, I gave him what he asked for instead of what he needed.

He was asking for thoughts to help change emotions, and that normally doesn't work. But I was fatigued. So I gave him strategy. Not surprisingly, it did him little to no good.

I knew I had to think *differently*. I got above my own thinking and realized that his anger was birthed from pain, and his pain needed connection and empathy, far more than his anger needed strategy. I mustered all my emotional stamina and began to lean into his pain. As I connected with him and expressed empathy, he slowed down. After a few moments, his heart softened, and he had an epiphany of what had been driving his anger.

"Thinking" is a rich palette of options, especially when we consider that most people operate from a single thought process, and innumerable options are available. Thinking includes reason, deduction, intuition, memorization, integration, improvisation, synthesis, reflection, and many other processes.

If you are wondering why the change you are seeking eludes you, consider that perhaps thinking another *thing* cannot help and that, instead, you need to think another *way*.

The move from one thought process to another can be a challenge. Try these steps to see things in a new way. When you are stuck, trying to solve a problem, or simply need a fresh set of eyes, try these six strategies, the six S's:

1. **Stop**. Often, the forward momentum of our thought process keeps us from shifting. Take a moment to clear your mind.

2. **Shift**. Use your brain in some way other than the type of thinking that has you stuck. If you are trying to do something detailed, shift to something *creative*. When you come back, you might find that your mind has loosened.

3. **See**. See things from another perspective. Look at your situation through another person's eyes or from a different angle. Consider how someone of the opposite sex might see the issue, or someone from another culture. See through the eyes of someone older or someone younger.

4. **Slow**. While our culture encourages speed, the mind does not shift well at high speed. New thought processes must be cultivated, not driven. Slow down.

5. **Share**. Consider collaborating to help your mind stretch. Bring in anoth-

er perspective or set of skills.

6. **Settle**. Settle down on the inside. The more anxiety we feel, the less access we have to the higher functions of the brain.

Slow down, look through new eyes, and discover just how much more your mind wants to show you!

The mind carries out its assignment without even asking your permission. Your mind is trying to take the mountain of data coming in through your senses and make your world manageable. Rather than let your mind do this without your guidance, make your mind your ally, not your obstacle. Take charge. Think about thinking, and learn the language of your mind.

Remember, our capacity to think about thinking is a superpower.

"Thinking: the talking of the soul with itself."

—Plato

Think is written by Bob Hamp

"The greatest moments in life are not concerned with selfish achievements but rather with the things we do for the people we love and esteem, and whose respect we need."

—Walt Disney

Thoughtful

thought·ful

/ˈTHôtfəl/

Adjective

1. *Absorbed in or involving thought*

2. *Showing consideration for the needs of other people*

3. *Showing careful consideration or attention*

I recently heard a story about a leader at Walt Disney World Parks and Resorts who took the time to learn some very simple things about her cast members that would lead to more meaningful employee relationships.

Walt Disney World employs thousands of college students for short-term internships. This particular leader wanted to know, if there was one magical experience that she could grant to each intern under her responsibility, what would it be?

As the interns turned in their biographies, along with their goals and desired experiences, this leader systematically began to create these magical moments for each of her interns, one by one. The end result of her being *thoughtful*: a culture of commitment and trust.

When leaders are thoughtful in their approach to their employees, they can change the culture of their businesses, both internally and externally. You see, customers can feel the climate of an organization without ever speaking to someone.

I have heard it said that leaders are like a thermostat: they can create an environment that is frustrating and stressful through heat. They can also create one that is cold and callous through passivity and isolation. Or they can keep the temperature just right, with a balance of drive and support.

The only way you are going to know where to find the sweet spot is by knowing your people, both personally and professionally. This is what the thoughtful leader is all about. Where you kick it up a notch is by deciding how you might be able to help each of your employees achieve his or her dreams in life. That is truly being thoughtful.

Your challenge this week is to get to know your employees. What are their hopes and dreams? What can you do to help them achieve those hopes and dreams? Start making progress as soon as you can. I assure you, the moment word gets out that you've taken a genuine interest in those who work for you and you're backing it up with action, things are going to change around the office—for the better.

"Thoughtfulness for others, generosity, modesty, and self-respect are the qualities which make a real gentleman or lady."

—Thomas Huxley

Thoughtful is written by Jon Langford

"Time is what we want most,
but what we use worst."

—William Penn

Time

time

/tīm/

Noun

1. *The indefinite continued progress of existence and events in the past, present, and future regarded as a whole*

2. *A point of time as measured in hours and minutes past midnight or noon*

Verb

1. *Plan, schedule, or arrange when (something) should happen or be done*

2. *Measure the time taken by (a process or activity, or a person doing it)*

You've heard of the power of *compound interest* and likely experienced it either in a positive or negative way when trying to save money. Einstein even called it the eighth wonder of the world. What is the most powerful element of compound interest? *Time.* The earlier you begin the process of saving, the more growth can happen!

Finances are important and can bring tremendous returns over time, but what has even more potential for impact with the right investments? People. The impact you can have by investing your most precious resource (time) into people is what I call *compound influence*.

We are all the result of the influence of many, but in my story, *one* person took the time to teach, train, encourage, and develop me as a leader for three years, from when I was eighteen until I turned twenty-one. That season marked my life and helped me see that I had significant potential to make a difference in the lives of others. For the thirteen years since then, I've lived a very different life because of that time of development.

My mentor impacted three actual years of my life, and therefore human history. But if I live to be one hundred years old, you could say he impacted eighty-two years of human history because my life will never be the same. Yet it goes far deeper than that. I've had the chance, over the past thirteen years, to invest in hundreds of other lives, as he did in mine. When you've been given a gift, the most rewarding thing in the world is to give it away!

The math is easy. If I impact only an average of ten lives per year, and those people have an average of fifty years of life remaining, I have the chance to impact more than 41,000 years of human history. Talk about a return on investment! That's not even considering the impact those people have on others.

Considering compound influence changes the way we have conversations with our coworkers, sit in staff meetings, and invest in young leaders at our companies; it also impacts the way we see our own children. If you can believe in someone, speak potential into them, and help them grasp the power of the time they've been given, you can truly leave a legacy of change with the days you have been given.

Here are five key principles that can help you capitalize on your time to create compound influence:

1. Reflect on how people have used their time to impact your life.

2. Consider who in your circle of influence you can develop.

3. Remember that time is the scarcest and most valuable asset we have. Most everything else can be replaced in some way…but not time.

4. Schedule how you will use time intentionally today to move others forward.

5. Remove aspects of your calendar that aren't bringing you a solid return.

"The cost of a thing is the amount of what I will call life which is required to be exchanged for it, immediately or in the long run."

—Henry David Thoreau

Time is written by Aaron Kruse

"You have to be transparent so you no longer cast a shadow but instead let the light pass through you."

—**Kamand Kojouri**

Transparency

trans·par·en·cy

/ˌtranˈsperənsē/

Noun

1. *The condition of being transparent*

2. *An image, text, or positive transparent photograph printed on transparent plastic or glass, able to be viewed using a projector*

The word *transparency* sums up one of the keys to my success as a television host on the world's number one electronic retailer, QVC. By putting transparency into place as a part of my product presentations, I was able to sell almost $4 billion worth of merchandise during my twenty-nine-year career.

I'll never forget the pivotal moment when the importance of transparency became crystal clear to me (forgive the play on words.) I was presenting a set of nonstick cookware. I had prepared a pasta dish in a large skillet, and as I began to transfer it onto a plate, the pasta went flying over the plate and onto the studio floor! The director instructed the cameraman not to show it, but I knew the viewers had already seen the pasta miss the plate.

To the director's chagrin, I walked out in front of the counter and called for the camera to come in tight for a close-up of the pile of pasta on the floor. I then laughed at myself and said that this was a common occurrence in my kitchen at home. I told the viewers that I often made a mess in the kitchen whenever I tried to cook. There was no denying how slippery the nonstick pan was, so I emphasized that they would never have to worry about food sticking to their cookware again!

After the show, I was bombarded with emails from viewers. (Yes, this was before Facebook existed!) The viewers loved the fact that I showed them the mess I had made and that I admitted that I missed the plate. They also loved that I told them I was not a very good cook. That day, many people told me they totally related to me because they weren't good in the kitchen, either. While most of them enjoyed the humor of my mistake, they absolutely loved the fact that I didn't try to hide it!

A light bulb turned on inside my brain. I realized that by being honest and transparent, I had built up their trust in me. It was one of the most important lessons I learned about sales and life. By admitting my mistake, drawing attention to it, and laughing at myself, I was able to turn my mistake into one of my best moments in front of the television camera. I made many mistakes after that, but I always pointed them out and had fun admitting my humanness.

We tend to go into protection mode when we feel like somebody is trying to "sell" us. Subconsciously, we put our hands over our wallets to keep our money safe. The goal of a great salesperson is to have people take out their wallets, give you their money, and feel great about doing it. This doesn't happen until you, the salesperson, build trust with the customer. It is extremely important to be real, and to be real, you have to be transparent.

From that day on, transparency became a watchword for me. It is not only a key to success in the sales world, but in any business or personal relationship. People know when you are being real. Transparency is the key to being trustworthy.

It takes courage to let people see you for who you really are. But transparency leads to trust in any relationship, whether it is with your boss, your employee, your spouse, your child, or your friend. For people to fully love you, they must fully trust you first.

Even the Bible tells us that transparency is not an option. The book of John says, "And ye shall know the truth, and the truth shall set you free." Most people are afraid to let the world know who they truly are. They tend to hide behind the image they present on the job, on social media, and to other people. Everyone seems to be more concerned about how they are perceived than who they really are.

Here are three practical ways to weave transparency into your life:

1.   Take control of your tendency to cover up your mistakes.

2.   Think about what you are going to say before you say it. Make sure you are being truthful.

3.   Recognize when your pride tries to keep you from being totally transparent.

Just as light shines through transparent objects, so truth shines through transparent people. Let's let the truth shine us each and every day.

"Speak the truth. Transparency breeds legitimacy."
—John C. Maxwell

Transparency is written by Dan Wheeler

*"The best way to find out if you can trust
somebody is to trust them."*

—Ernest Hemingway

/trəst/

Noun

1. *Firm belief in the reliability, truth, ability, or strength of someone or something*

2. *(Law) An arrangement whereby a person (a trustee) holds property as its nominal owner for the good of one or more beneficiaries*

Verb

1. *Believe in the reliability, truth, ability, or strength of*

Trust. It's a word we hear regularly.

People cry that we need to rebuild trust in government, business, and communities. It's a crisis that plays out in the evening news and with every new scandal that is reported.

And trust is a much bigger issue in the smallest places in our lives as it plays out throughout the day. It begins within each of us in small places, where trust is unattended to or just assumed. You see, we were created for relationships, and trust is the foundation of those relationships.

Consider the following statements in which people voice their frustration about various situations:

- "You are not listening to me, and it's clear you don't really care. Time after time, you have left my needs subject to your convenience. I'll find someone who truly cares about their customers!"

- "Day in and day out, I put in my time, get no feedback or opportunities, and I never know what's happening. You just assume that I am here to make your life better and never consider what your decisions cost me. I quit this miserable job!"

- "You do not understand how I am feeling. Everything you say is either thoughtless or just plain hurtful. And you never keep the promises you make. You haven't heard anything I said. Night after night, it's like I am talking to a wall, if you're even here at all. I want a divorce—*now*!"

- "Yeah? Whatever! You suck! I hate you, Dad!"

- "Nobody cares! I can't take the pressure, and I don't think anyone would miss me if I were gone."

What do all these phrases, or perhaps the long and painful experience of silence, have in common? They illustrate a loss of trust, or the trust gap between people, or even within yourself. That gap is painful and upsetting and can lead to disastrous results.

The wider the trust gap, the further away a person will drift...until he or she is ultimately gone. That gap can be lethal, and you might have just a moment to switch the direction, close the gap, and transform the relationship.

The good news is that intentional and mindful efforts to cultivate trust will transform your relationships, and it can start as soon as you take action.

It's the little things that matter when building trust, especially when little things are done consistently over time. Small deposits of trust build interest and eventually become great vaults of trust. Here is how you build those riches:

1. **Be trustworthy, and build trust from the inside out.** It begins when you live with integrity and can truly trust *yourself.* This begins the transformation in how we live.

2. **Be authentic, and take responsibility for your relationships**. We need to be humble in trying to understand others, attending to the little things, and cultivating transparency in our personal relationships.

3. **Be dependable, keep your promises, and communicate consistently.** The experience others have with you will be defined by your performance and how you manage expectations.

4. **Be influential, be a good steward of trust, and make a difference in the lives of people around you.** Give trust only to those who deserve it, and when someone trusts you, do good things with it.

That is how we can eliminate the trust gap.

"To be trusted is a greater compliment than being loved."

— George MacDonald

Trust is written by Roy Reid

"I waited patiently for the Lord; he turned to me and heard my cry. He lifted me out of the slimy pit, out of the mud and mire; He set my feet on a rock and gave me a firm place to stand."

—Psalm 40:1–2 (NIV)

Unstuck

un·stuck

/ˌənˈstək/

Adjective

1. *Past and past participle of unstick*

Have you ever been driving a vehicle that got stuck? If so, you know how frustrating it can be. However, spinning your wheels in a vehicle, buried in the mud, barely compares to a *life* that has lost traction.

A few years ago, I found myself wondering if I was still on the right career path. The malaise might as well have been mud. Many days, I felt hopeless as I struggled through the mundane monotony, with little hope of renewal at work. Admittedly, there were times that being stuck in my career also affected other areas of my life.

Looking back, I could have settled for the status quo and stayed stuck. Many people make that choice. How about you? Do you feel trapped in a dead-end job, dreading the drudgery of work? Are you merely going through the motions in your relationships with those who matter most? Are you mired in a habit you need to break?

If you answered *yes* to any of those, there is good news. You can become *unstuck*. A fulfilling and significant career is still possible. Your most important relationships can again be life-giving and bring you joy. And your life can experience transformation as you leave destructive habits behind and redirect yourself toward growth.

When we are bogged down, our inclination is to grind it out and try harder. But if you have ever had a vehicle that was stuck, you know that pushing the accelerator only buries you deeper in the muck. After discovering that trying harder doesn't work, the temptation can shift to trying less and choosing to disengage. Trying less might feel easier, but it fails to create progress. The only thing that helps when you are stuck is to gain traction.

Fortunately, there is a formula you can apply to help you gain traction:

Introspection
+ Redirection
+ Action
= Traction

It begins with *introspection*—looking inside yourself. In today's world of increased regulations, most of us are used to the concept of *inspection*. We constantly inspect our work systems and processes to ensure that our employees are safe and our customers are well served. But do you spend time inspecting what's inside—inspecting your heart?

Deliberately inspecting your life has power. Through *introspection*, you examine what's going on inside you and around you. You allow curiosity to become your friend. You step back and work through your sacred questions. You pay attention to how you feel and what you think about things. In essence, you develop the skill of listening to your life. It is there that you gain clarity concerning the person you want to be and the life you want to live.

Introspection will tell you where your life needs to change.

After introspection comes *redirection*. Redirection is defined as assigning or directing something to a new or different place or purpose. As you recognize adjustments you need to make, you will need to redirect some areas of your life.

Imagine you are driving a car, and you realize you are heading in the wrong direction. You are driving east but should be heading west. It is not enough to *recognize* you are going in the wrong direction. It is not enough to just slow down. And it is not enough to stop the car. You must turn the car around and point it in a different direction. That's the shift *redirection* calls for. It is unleashing your will on an area of life and creating a new compass setting.

Introspection + Redirection is only part of the formula. Once you've pointed the car in the right direction, you must put your foot on the gas pedal and move. That's *action*. Action is the process of actually doing something. You have come to the realization that things aren't right and decide on a new direction—now you need to take specific actions that will get you there.

Patiently working the Traction Formula will result in the needed *traction* to move you down the road toward renewal.

Working the formula and *becoming* unstuck is great, but *staying* unstuck is the goal. I took the following three concrete steps to regain traction in my life. I'm convinced they will help you stay engaged and unstuck, too:

1. **Define.** The first thing I had to do was define what I wanted. This was a process that started with paying attention to who I am. I asked myself defining questions like "Where is the energy?" "Where is the effectiveness?" "What is the need I can meet?" and "Where is the affirmation?" These questions all helped me identify my preferred future. These sacred questions can help you gain clarity about where you are and where you need to redirect.

2. **Align**. The next thing I did was line my life up with what I had defined. I remind myself often, "My direction always determines my destination." And so does yours. Every time I took a baby step, I found myself closer to where I wanted to be.

Like me, you must align your actions with *your* target. If you're not willing to do whatever it takes to walk toward your dream, you likely have a lack of passion, which probably means you are focusing on the wrong target. I knew I had discovered my dream because my defining questions were answered. I was effective, energized, and able to meet a need, and people kept encouraging (and even paying) me.

3. **Refine**. Step three is to keep refining. For me, this included narrowing my focus, and more importantly, working on myself. As the process unfolded, I kept making adjustments. The challenge was that it required massive amounts of time, energy, thinking, questioning, and failing.

A fully engaged life is yours for the taking. If you will inspect your inner life often, redirect as needed, and live with a bias for action, you will be on your way to traction.

It's time for you to live *unstuck*!

"Vision without traction is merely hallucination."

—Gino Wickman,

Traction: Get a Grip on Your Business

Unstuck is written by Randy Gravitt

"Keep your thoughts positive because your thoughts become your words. Keep your words positive because your words become your behavior. Keep your behavior positive because your behavior becomes your habits. Keep your habits positive because your habits become your values. Keep your values positive because your values become your destiny."

—Mahatma Gandhi

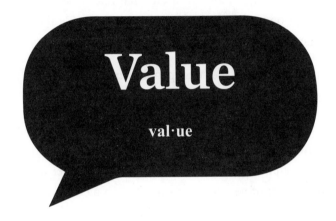

/ˈvalyo͞o/

Noun

1. *The regard that something is held to deserve; the importance, worth, or usefulness of something*

2. *A person's principles or standards of behavior; one's judgment of what is important in life*

Verb

1. *Estimate the monetary worth of (something)*

2. *Consider (someone or something) to be important or beneficial; have a high opinion of*

What does *value* mean to you? Is it just the price of something? Some expensive things are actually not valuable, if you really think about it.

Have you ever tried to shop for the basics—bread, milk, and eggs—when a bad storm is brewing? When the shelves are bare, you might have to stand outside the store and wait for those items while also paying double and triple what they normally cost. Why? Because they are now at a higher value than when the sun is shining and there is no desperate need for them. The thought of not having them seems to cause people to do whatever they can to get the items of survival. Well, I know for a fact that relationships with people in our lives and our own self-worth are even more valuable than that last loaf of bread on the shelf.

People are important to me: new people I meet, my family, my friends, and the people I interact with in my work.

I am an *extremely* outgoing person. I have never met a stranger. Going out into a crowd of people is comfortable for me. Going into a large mass of people, my common goal is to leave there having met new people and growing my network of people. I consider myself a connisseur of people, if you will. I value networking, connections, and growth.

Family time is everything to me. My parents are divorced, and sadly, our family members are spread out all around the United States. My time with them is rare, but man, when I am with them, it makes my heart sing. I value quality time with my family.

Also, the relationships I have built with friends, whether new or old, have become a vital part of who I am. I can't go a day without talking to a few of my closest friends to discuss life, love, and other mysteries. I make sure to maintain constant communication even with those who live a world away from me. I value my friendships and knowing someone is there for me to depend on in the easy and the hard times.

My job is something I sort of fell into. I worked retail for fifteen years and then was introduced to digital marketing. It was like a light bulb just flicked on in my mind. Everything made sense, and I uncovered a passion I never knew existed. I value my job and a company that believed in me enough to get me to where I am now.

In a world where everyone is so negative about literally everything, positivity is scarce, and positivity in our values is even more unusual. Being a people pleaser, I have always thought about how I can make others happy, ensure they are enjoying their time, and help them feel valued. But sometimes I forget to fuel *myself* and confirm that I am happy, enjoying my time, and making sure I feel valued.

I find myself on Instagram or other social media sites, following people like Gary Vee or Jay Shetty to help fuel my motivation and help me find value in my day. I will read a quote I have seen so many times before about knowing my worth and striving for more and convince myself that "Yes! This is what I needed today…" but then I won't apply it to my life due to distraction or pure laziness. I find myself in the same life-sucking hole the next day, in need of a motivational-quote boost.

I have realized that I place value on everyone and everything else, but what value am I applying to myself? Do I truly value who I am, who I have become, and who I intend to be?

To remedy this imbalance, I have started not only reading those quotes, but then allowing them to truly soak in and applying them to my life.

One of my favorite quotes is from Oscar Wilde: "Nowadays, people know the price of everything and the value of nothing." We are so concerned with monetary costs, but what we value might actually be free, such as time, experiences, and relationships.

When I think about the value of something, I often think about what is something worth. When you value something, it is worth so much more! For example, my Nana passed away about fifteen years ago. When she passed, my Papa gave me her owl collection. To others, it is just a group of owl figurines, but to me, it is a memory of her incredible spirit and how she was always so wise and always knew the right answer. They aren't worth much, but to me, they mean the world. Every time I have moved, I have put them in a special box to ensure they are safe, not to be harmed by someone with clumsy hands.

We do whatever we can to make sure we protect what is valuable to us, so what are we doing to protect the value of ourselves?

One of my favorite mantras is from *The Help*: "You is kind. You is smart. You is important."

Here are four things I do regularly to find value in myself. Do them on your own, and see how the value you place on yourself changes:

1. **Set priority to yourself.** Remember your needs, goals, and desires. Pamper yourself, go for a run, read a book, rest and relax.

2. **Set and maintain boundaries.** Know the value you bring to the table. Don't allow others to treat you less than you're worth.

3. **Set goals.** Don't just walk through life day by day; set goals that are attainable daily, weekly, monthly, and yearly. Give yourself something to strive toward.

4. **Set purpose in your actions.** When you make a decision, make it with pride. Make decisions according to what is best for you and your family.

"Nowadays people know the price of everything and the value of nothing."

—Oscar Wilde

Value is written by Candace Gingrasso

"Worry never robs tomorrow of its sorrow, it only saps today of its joy."

—Leo F. Buscaglia

Worry

wor·ry

/ˈwərē/

Verb

1. *Give way to anxiety or unease; allow one's mind to dwell on difficulty or troubles*

2. *(Of a dog or other carnivorous animal) Tear at, gnaw on, or drag around with the teeth*

Noun

1. *A state of anxiety and uncertainty over actual or potential problems*

I once heard it said that *worry* is paying interest on debt you might not owe. To fully function to the best of our ability, we must be fully focused in the *now* moment. The number one cause for accidents on jobsites is a lack of focus. It is impossible to be in a state of worry and still be focused, in the *now* moment.

Two polar-opposite things cannot possess the same space in time. In other words, it cannot be day and night at the same moment. And you cannot be in two different states at the same time—unless you are physically standing on the state line with one foot in one state and the other foot in another. You cannot be grateful and a victim at the same moment.

As I slowly learn Spanish, I learn a lot about English. There is much Latin in our vocabulary. The Spanish word for "worry" is *preocupado*. The word in Spanish helps us understand what worry does to us: it keeps us preoccupied. Worry keeps us from being fully present, fully functioning in the now moment. It also causes our bodies to release chemicals that cause us to feel bad, increase acid in our system, take away our focus, and turn a protective mental state from a resource to a burden.

In the study of *epigenetics*, we learn that each of us is a community of 300 trillion cells, all driven by our environment. The most important environment that controls us is our thinking. The body releases sixty-three known chemicals. What we are thinking about—what is going on in our heads and hearts—dictates how we feel and how we function. Our thoughts can either be a positive motivator that propels us forward, with hope, or they can be a negative drain on our emotional and physical health and thus affect our ability to function and our belief systems. When we worry, we cause our bodies to release chemicals related to doubt, fear, and uncertainty.

If we are going to function at the highest levels of our design, we must learn how to focus on the right things and do our best to remove worry. Dr. Stephen Covey, in his seminal book *The 7 Habits of Highly Effective People*, talks about the two circles of life: the circle of concern and the circle of influence. He tells us that we should keep our focus on where those two circles overlap. Within the circle of *influence* are those things we can control or affect. Within the circle of *concern* are those things we are concerned about. Where they overlap is where our focus should be.

When we worry, we are running scenarios of things that might happen and have negative consequences. As leaders, we need to be prepared for whatever situations might occur. However, worry is the creative process, in the negative sense, running on its own and creating chemicals in our bodies that cause our minds to go places they should not go and causing our bodies to release chemicals that make us sick, anxious, or hopeless. Those feelings do not motivate us; they demotivate us from taking action because they affect our B.S. (belief system).

In her book *Who Switched Off My Brain?* Dr. Caroline Leaf makes this statement that should wake up every able-minded leader: "Research shows that around 87 percent of illnesses can be attributed to our thought life and approximately 13 percent to diet, genetics, and environment. Studies conclusively link more chronic diseases (also known as lifestyle diseases) to an epidemic of toxic proportions in our culture. These toxic emotions can cause migraines, hypertension, strokes, cancer, skin problems, diabetes, infections, and allergies, just to name a few. Despite all the marvels of modern high-tech medicine and decades of innovative research, these illnesses are increasing worldwide."

How do we combat these menacing mental mitigators? By taking control of our thoughts, we hold them captive. To think is to create, and we must be aware of what we are creating through the automatic thoughts that run through our brains on a moment-by-moment basis.

Here are some tips for controlling your thoughts:

1. **Check in with your thoughts daily.** In the morning and in the evening, journal your thoughts. Pay attention to what you are focused on. Become aware of the pattern of your thoughts. Are they worrisome, or are they solution-oriented?

2. **Separate your thoughts into two categories: things you are concerned about and things you have the ability to control or have an effect on.** Focus your attention on where those two overlap.

3. **Remember that there are two ways to change something.** You either have unilateral authority to change things, or you can help effect change by talking with others to find out their concerns and then strategize on how to change those things that you are not satisfied with.

4. **Regarding those things that occupy a lot of time and space, put to-gether a plan to solve, fix, or reduce your concerns in relation to them.** When we have a plan in place, it makes us feel like we are in control, and it reduces the worry and fear.

If I could be like Michael J. Fox and go "back to the future" and tell a younger me a bit of advice, I would tell that little me, "Be careful what you hold on to." For years, I struggled with worry. The preoccupation of what might happen, what might go wrong, what might crash kept me from focus-ing on creating a better future. Now that I hold my thoughts captive, I can plan and prepare without putting myself through all the emotions associated with negative possibilities that are all outside of the realm of my control.

Over the years, I have learned that true power lies between the stimulus and the response. Dr. Viktor Frankl, the father of Logotherapy, says, "Be-tween the stimulus and the response, there is a space, and in that space is your power; it is your freedom." That is true power—to control one's own mind and thus the chemicals and feelings that come from what we do in the recesses of our minds.

Take control, take back your power, and live in the quiet freedom that can be your mind.

> *"That the birds of worry and care fly over your head, you cannot change, but that they build nests in your hair, this you can prevent."*
>
> **—Chinese Proverb**

Worry is written by Scott V. Black

Darrell Amy

Author, Revenue Growth Engine

Darrell Amy is a trailblazer, passionate about helping people and organizations grow. As the author of *Revenue Growth Engine*, he helps great businesses double revenue by aligning marketing and sales enablement. Passionate about value and authenticity, Darrell co-hosts the *Selling From the Heart* podcast. He founded Convergo, a marketing and sales enablement agency serving technology resellers across North America. He serves as the Executive Director of the ManAlive EXPEDITION, an initiative to help men discover their hearts. He also co-chairs the Kingdom Missions Fund, providing venture capital to innovative missions projects. Darrell and his wife Leslie live in Conway, Arkansas where they enjoy time with their three children and three grandchildren. During down time, you can find Darrell on the lake in his sailboat or hiking in the Ozark mountains

Connect with Darrell:

(501) 626-4110

www.convergomarketing.com

www.sellingfromtheheart.net/podcast-home

Alex Anderson

VP of Relate Coaching, Founder of My Core Motivations

Alex serves as a Senior Associate Pastor at Bayside Community Church in Bradenton/Sarasota, Florida. In 2011, Outreach Magazine named the church as the tenth-fastest-growing church in America. He writes the monthly "Spiritual Wellness" column for *Southwest Florida Health and Wellness Magazine* and is the author of the book, *Dangerous Prayers: You Will Never*

Look at Prayer the Same.

Alex has been married to his wife and best friend, Kim, for more than thirty-two years. Together (mostly Kim) they eventually raised three children. He has been a minister for more than forty years, but don't hold that against him; he was also a businessman for eighteen of those years. Alex and Kim make their home in Bradenton, Florida.

Connect with Alex:

(941) 228-7634

alex@alexanderson.com

www.mybayside.church

www.mycoremotivations.com

Dr. Chris Auger

Program Consultant, WinShape Teams, retired Naval Seal commander

Dr. Auger currently serves as a program consultant with WinShape Teams under the umbrella of the WinShape Foundation founded by Truett Cathy of Chick-fil-A.

He earned his Doctorate from Regent University in Strategic Leadership with a concentration in Leadership Coaching. After almost twenty-eight years on US Navy SEAL teams, he also earned a master's degree in Global Leadership from the University of San Diego and a bachelor's degree in Information Systems Management from the University of Maryland University College.

Dr. Auger is a Board-Certified Coach through the Center for Credentialing and Education and has been formally conducting performance coaching since 2013. He specializes in servant leadership, emotional intelligence,

DiSC profiles, and experiential learning. He enjoys life with his bride of twenty-seven years and his only daughter and her husband, not to mention their dog, a Jack Russell/pug mix. It is Dr, Auger's goal to serve and help others achieve significance.

Connect with Dr. Chris:

(678) 283-7522, WinShape Teams

Cauger@winshape.org

www.winshape.org

Scott V. Black

CEO, Like It Matters

Scott is a radio host and coach for Like It Matters leadership-development events. He strives to help organizations and individuals maximize the potential they were created with. He is the ultimate life-caddy, motivator, and change agent. He is certified as a Human Behavioral Specialist, a Chaplain and Drug and Alcohol counselor, and he is a Master Practitioner of Neuro Linguistic Programming (NLP), specializing in EQ (Emotional Intelligence), TA (Transactional Analysis), CBT(Cognitive Behavioral Therapy), and MI (Multiple Intelligences).

For more than twenty-seven years, Scott has conducted Transformational Leadership training across three countries. He has impacted tens of thousands of clients and their lives have been enriched, educated, and informed by Mr. Black's trainings, education and inspiration. He continues to hold his famous transitional leadership-training classes across the nation and provides executive and life coaching. His Leadership Awakening course is nationally recognized as the most powerful leadership training available today.

Scott also hosts his own radio show, *Like It Matters Radio! LIM Radio* airs daily from 9 to 10 a.m. Central Standard Time on iHeart Radio-search, Wellness Radio 1570. LIM Radio is also available on iTunes, Stitcher, TuneIn, and the website likeitmattersradio.com. *LIM Radio* has fans all over the world who tune in daily to hear the inspiring leadership principles and teachings that only Scott can offer. "Inspirational, Educational, and Applicational" are the core values of the Hour of Power.

Scott and his beautiful bride, Valerie, live in the Dallas–Fort Worth, Texas area with their four children: Faith, Christian, Major, and Benaiah.

Connect with Scott:

(817) 657-4921

Mr.Black@LikeItMatters.net

likeitmattersradio.com

likeitmatters.net

Donna Bosmeny

Vice President of Human Resources and Administration, Success for All

Foundation

The Success for All Foundation (SFAF) is a nonprofit educational reform based in Baltimore, Maryland. Donna began her career in human resources in the banking industry and, after raising two sons and successfully building her own design business, she returned to her first career in human resources. A self-proclaimed process geek, she enjoys the daily changes in an HR arena.

While she continues to work for her Baltimore nonprofit organization and provide leadership, she resides in the Sarasota, Florida area with her husband, Alan. She has two incredible sons, two amazing daughters-in-law, and four grandchildren who take her breath away.

Her personal philosophy in life is to be sure not to sweat the small stuff, to live without regret, and to seize the day, every day.

Connect with Donna:

dbosmeny@successforall.org

www.successforall.org

Noble Bowman

Business Coach with Rhapsody Coaching

Nobel has spent most of his life working with leaders to help them achieve their potential—both professionally and personally. Over the past twenty years, he had the opportunity to lead several organizations. He knows what it's like to drive revenue, realign culture, develop strategy, and implement solutions that work. He knows—firsthand—the life of an entrepreneur and organizational leader.

Nobel has the privilege of being the Chaplin for the Missouri State Bears basketball, volleyball, and softball teams. His personal style will seem like he is talking just to you. He loves to say, "You coach people and teams one at a time."

Sometimes he is delivering keynotes around the world. Other times, he is working one-on-one with a leader. Either way, he wants you to know this: the work you are doing is important, the commitment you've made to yourself and your organization matters, and the opportunities ahead of you are extraordinary.

Nobel and his wife, Kesia, have three boys and live in Springfield, Missouri.

Connect with Nobel:

(417) 496-9077

noblebowman@gmail.com

rhapsodystrategies.com

Michael Bray

Entrepreneur/Chief Visionary, Business Strategist

Michael has more than forty years of business venture in his history. He was referred to as the "Golden Nugget" in several businesses along the years. Michael started off working with Clint Murchison (former owner of the Dallas Cowboys) and became the youngest VP of sales and marketing in Murchison's firm. It was there he learned how to do things right in a big way.

Since then, Michael has revolutionized business, developing Lexxus, a wellness company. He took it public and achieved more than $1 billion in annual sales. He owns US City Energy, a Tesla Technology company that increases efficiency through solar energy. He also owns Global Pocket Media, which puts ads in everyone's pockets. His latest venture is Ancestry Genetics, which provides revolutionary prescreening testing for early detection of hereditary diseases.

Michael says only a dreamer can change the dream. He lives in central Arkansas.

Connect with Michael:

(501) 247-5189

unleashedwealth@gmail.com

Brian Buckley

Senior Vice President, IOA Insurance; Founder, Better Man Event

Brian founded a nonprofit organization called Better Man Ministries in 2004. In 2005, he and a few of his friends started a Better Man Event (BME). The event has grown from an initial attendance of forty-eight to thousands every year at the BME.

Over these past fourteen years, thousands of men have come to be better husbands, dads, brothers, neighbors, leaders, and friends by attending a three-hour power-packed event with nationally recognized speakers. These coaches of life tell their stories about how they became better, inspiring others to do the same. Brian is in love with his wife of thirty-four years, Lorrie Ann. They are proud of their son, David, and live in central Florida.

Connect with Brian:

(407) 341-4043

Brian.buckley@ioausa.com

bettermanministries.com

www.ioausa.com

Kennan Burch

CEO, Brand Catalyst Partners

Kennan, a former Director of Marketing for Red Lobster, is a brand architect who inspires CEOs and leadership teams to align with and live their highest promise. His efforts focus on training the employees and upper-level managers of organizations.

Brand Catalyst Partners has been active for more than ten years and has now partnered with CEOs (Brand Catalysts) in almost every sector of business, including restaurants, boat manufacturers, insurance companies, retail stores, organic products, financial institutions, law firms, digital content providers, creative agencies, commercial real estate development, schools, coffee shops, financial services, accounting, security services, retail products, surface design, surface distribution, dry cleaning, theme parks, product design, metal fabrication, hotels, athletic teams, interior design, mediation, water parks, business transition firms, self-publishing, business publications, waste removal, office automation, CEO groups, bowl games, musicians, media campaigns, athletes, reality shows, entertainment, churches, and nonprofit organizations.

Kennan his wife, Lyn, have three children and live in Winter Garden, Florida.

Connect with Kennan:

(407) 654-7008

kennan@brandcatalystpartners.com

brandcatalystpartners.com

Edgar Cabello

Leadership Development, Lippert Components (RV Products Division)

Edgar has more than twenty-five years of leadership experience. As senior pastor of an innovative multicultural congregation in South Bend, Indiana he helped shape an environment that blended people from a variety of ethnic and socioeconomic backgrounds.

Also, he has helped develop more than a dozen church start-ups with a focus on board development and "key leader" training.

Currently, Edgar serves as one of the leadership development directors at Lippert Components, a publicly traded manufacturing company with more than 12,000 teammates. He coaches and guides leaders and teams of leaders, focusing on companies' core values and leader qualities.

Edgar is an avid reader, podcast junkie, and hiker who holds a degree in communications from Indiana University. He and his wife, Cynthia, have four grown sons and three grandchildren and reside in South Bend, Indiana.

Connect with Edgar:

(574) 532-6360

ecabello@lci1.com

www.lci1.com

Joe Calamusa IV

Director of Sales Training, University of Alabama

Joe is currently the Managing Director of The University of Alabama (UA) Sales Program and a Clinical Professor of Marketing in the Culverhouse College of Commerce.

Before joining the UA faculty, Joe spent ten years as the Corporate National Sales Manager for Peco Foods, Inc., a privately held and fully integrated poultry processor. While at Peco, he started a private-label grocery division that blossomed into more than $150 million in annual sales to retail giants such as Walmart, The Kroger Co., Supervalu Inc., Safeway, Publix, Dollar General, and many others. At Peco, Joe oversaw a national sales and broker network and was responsible for the division's strategy, supply chain, product development, and profitability.

Prior to working at Peco Foods, he served as a Brand Manager for the Bryan Foods division of Sara Lee Corp. In that role, he managed all product development, marketing, and sales support for the hams and canned-meats categories.

Joe holds a bachelor's degree and a Master of Business Administration degree from The University of Alabama. He is a cofounder and performer with the Sales & Leadership Development Group. His experience in corporate training and coaching span the consumer-packaged goods, health care, retail, media, industrial technology, and municipal segments. He also specializes in small-business consulting projects within the legal, information technology, and nonprofit fields.

Joe lives in Tuscaloosa, Alabama.

Connect with Joe:

(205) 348-8923

jcalamus@cba.ua.edu

www.joecalamusa.com

Chris Capehart

CMO, Oven Bits; Author

Chris's story is proof that although life rarely gives us what we hope for, we can still beat the odds and achieve a meaningful life. Every challenge presents a choice—to either let circumstances define us or to do exactly the opposite. Chris has made it a point to do exactly the opposite by defining his own life and taking purposeful steps to overcome every challenge thrown his way.

His fresh approach to overcoming the inevitable challenges life brings inspires and motivates people from all walks of life to connect with their purpose and move beyond the challenges they face. His experience of defying the odds stretches beyond overcoming personal challenges and into the business realm. Growing up, Chris worked in the family "start-up" business that went on to gross more than $200 million. In the years since, Chris has started or had ownership in more than ten businesses, experiencing a wide range of ups and downs—from losing everything to building it all back from scratch.

While serving as CMO at Oven Bits, Chris drove more than 100 percent growth, adding millions in revenue and helping produce more than twenty featured apps in the Apple and Google App Stores. He accomplished this in partnership with brands such as L'Oréal, Lush Cosmetics, Hilton, and Vogue. During this time, Chris published his first book, *Step: Pursuing Your Dreams in the Midst of Everyday Life.*

Chris has since produced *Life Story: A Step-by-Step Guide to Creating the Life You've Always Wanted*, *The "Blank" Leader: An In-Depth Guide to Becoming a Thriving Leader*, and *The Intentional Year: A Year Dedicated to Making You Unstoppable.*

Through the exhilarating heights of hard-earned success to the lows of disappointing failures, Chris has learned a handful of key principles that have helped him defeat the odds. He's now on a mission to teach people of all walks of life how they, too, can defeat the odds, no matter what their "everyday lives" look like.

Connect with Chris:

chris@chriscapehart.co

www.chriscapehart.co

ovenbits.com

Dr. Alicia Cotabish

Associate Professor, College of Education, University of Central Arkansas

Dr. Alicia Cotabish is an Associate Professor of Teaching and Learning at the University of Central Arkansas and the owner of Fretmonkey Records, the organized international community of fingerstyle guitar. In both roles, Alicia has established herself as a thought leader and entrepreneur.

In higher education, she has served on a number of boards and has published more than one hundred articles and books on education. In the music industry, Alicia has established Fretmonkey Records as an international music brand with monthly guitar nights in five countries and an office in China. With the concepts "community" and "collaboration" serving as her thought-leadership platform in both education and the music industry, Alicia has managed to be a "mover and shaker" in both fields. Alicia and her husband, Dennis, reside in Conway, Arkansas with their three children.

Connect with Dr. Alicia:

(501) 346-8228

acotabish@uca.edu

uca.edu

Lee Cockerell

Executive Vice President, Walt Disney World® Resort (Retired and Inspired)

Lee is the former Executive Vice President of Operations for the Walt Disney World® Resort. As the Senior Operating Executive for ten years, Lee led a team of forty thousand cast members and was responsible for the operations of twenty resort hotels, four theme parks, two water parks, a shopping and entertainment village, and the ESPN sports and recreation complex. He also was responsible for the ancillary operations which supported the number one vacation destination in the world.

Lee is the author of four best-selling books: *Creating Magic—10 Com-*

mon Sense Leadership Strategies, From a Life at Disney: The Customer Rules—The 39 Essential Rules for Delivering Sensational Service, Time Management Magic—How to Get More Done Every Day and Move from Surviving to Thriving, and *Career Magic—How to Stay on Track to Achieve a Stellar Career*.

He and his wife, Priscilla, live in Orlando, Florida.

Connect with Lee:

(407) 908-2118

Lee@LeeCockerell.com

www.leecockerell.com

Dr. Sam Farina

Executive Coach

Dr. Farina draws from years of church leadership and is well known for his dynamic and creative speaking ability. Believing in the possibilities and value coaching holds for emerging leaders motivated him to create The Farina Group, which is composed of specialists in the field of coaching. Dr. Farina has achieved the title of Professional Certified Coach with the International Coach Federation and focuses on executive, individual, and team coaching with the use of multiple assessments.

He holds a Doctor of Ministry degree with an emphasis in professional coaching.

After pioneering to create the Assemblies of God Coaching Network, Dr. Farina continues to train coaches for the network and serves on its coaching board and task force. He hosts a monthly Coaching Skills Webinar.

He and his wife, Vicki, who is an ACC Certified Coach, live in the Dallas, Texas metroplex. They are passionate about leading individuals, teams, and organizations to achieve their full potential.

Connect with Sam:

(919) 696-0184

Sfarina@samfarina.com

samfarina.com

Justin Flom

Master Magician

Justin has a magical life. After graduating from high school and spending a few years in Branson entertaining audiences, Justin began posting videos on YouTube, Instagram, Facebook, and anywhere else he could find an outlet online. The efforts paid off when the staff of Las Vegas Weekly named him "Best Up-and-Coming Entertainer" in their 2013 Weekly Awards. Fast-forward to today, and Justin has been viewed more than one billion times on his on platforms and others.

Today Justin is touring with country superstars Florida Georgia Line and creating magic for other stars and companies, including Coca-Cola, Hobby Lobby, Lady Antebellum, Super Bowl Coach Pete Carroll and the entire Seattle Seahawks team, John Legend, Nick Jonas, and Chrissy Teigen. Justin finds himself in front of as diverse an audience as any entertainer. His tours take him to buildings like Madison Square Garden to mega-churches and amphitheaters across the United States. He truly has the ability to entertain anyone, anywhere!

Justin has found a home in front of the lens. He has made regular appearances on Ellen, The Today Show, Racheal Ray, network late-night shows, on various shows with WWE Wrestling stars, and on his own show, *Wizard Wars*, for two seasons on SYFY.

In addition to national shows, Justin has starred in various commercials for Coke, American Airlines, CMT, and Kellogg's. He is the author of a children's book about magic, *Everyday Magic*, and is the coauthor of a book about his life, *Adventures of a Kid Magician*.

Connect with Justin:

Justin@Justinflom.com

www.justinflom.com

Candace Gingrasso

Digital Marketing Consultant

Candace is committed to being at the cutting edge of digital marketing and all it can bring to the business she serves. Her get-it-done attitude and keen sense for details make her a valuable asset to the marketing component of any business.

She enjoys watching movies, playing with dogs, planning events, and eating. In her spare time, she volunteers at Women and Children First: The Center Against Family Violence as the Vice President of the Peace Keepers. She also helps chair several local no-profit events such as the Easter Seals Fashion Event, WCF POP-Up Shop, and WCF Vegas on the Rocks.

Candace loves to entertain and is always looking for ways to host a party. Her goal in life is to have all the children and all the animals. She currently lives in West Palm Beach, Florida

Connect with Candace:

(501) 707-4974

candace.gingrasso@gmail.com

Chris Gingrasso

Founder, IMACT Freedom Inc.

Chris is a sales motivator, keynote speaker, and author who was raised in a small Wisconsin town. At the age of seven, he began doing magic professionally. His goal was to be a performer so people could forget about their troubles. Chris loves helping others experience healthy souls by engaging their emotions. He enjoys family, friends, and his faith.

Chris brings a vast background and experience as a sales leader, trainer, author, executive, business owner, speaker, nonprofit president, and most importantly, as a husband and a daddy. In his spare time, he and his wife, Heather, serve hurting children and their families in the foster-care system. They have five children and live in central Florida.

Connect with Chris:

(352) 989-2127

Gingrasso65@gmail.com

wowfactor.live

runfromtheedge.com

Randy Gravitt

CEO, Integreat Leadership

Randy is an author, speaker, and executive coach who encourages leaders to reach their potential.

In 2014, he founded Integreat Leadership, where he currently serves as the CEO, leading a team of coaches and consultants who work with high-performance leaders, organizations, and teams all over the world.

As a speaker, Randy delivers keynotes and training workshops on the topics of leadership, team building, organizational effectiveness, and peak performance. Those he works with include Chick-fil-A, Grand Hyatt, Fellowship of Christian Athletes, Kroger, and the WinShape Foundation. He served as a leadership coach for the Pittsburgh Pirates MLB Organization from 2013 to 2018.

Randy's writing includes two books he cowrote with Dan Webster, *Finding Your Way* and *UnSTUCK*. Both titles are aimed at helping leaders discover their passion and live fully engaged lives.

In his free time, Randy enjoys playing golf, reading, fishing, and traveling. He and his wife, Laura, live in Sharpsburg, Georgia and have four daughters.

Connect with Randy:

(678) 858-1167

randy@randygavitt.com

randygravitt.com

Bob Hamp

Founder, Think Differently Counseling

Bob is the founder of the Think Differently Counseling Consulting and Connecting Center. He has been in private practice and worked in the church for a combined twenty-five years of practice. Besides his years of private practice and organizational consulting, he spent ten years developing a group discipleship strategy called Freedom Ministry that helped thousands of people find freedom from a broad range of struggles.

He has published two books built around the idea that changing one's thought process is the true meaning of biblical repentance and, therefore, the key component of real change. His video series, Foundations of Freedom, is used worldwide to shift the way people see Christian views, themselves, and the pathway to change. He currently offers training and consulting to counselors, ministries, and curious people. He and his team offer training in facilitating freedom, spiritual leadership, teaching and training strategies, and ministry development.

Bob and his wife, Polly, have a wonderful blended family of six grown kids, two in-loves, and three awesome grandbabies. They live in the Dallas, Texas area.

Connect with Bob:

(972) 201-3437

hello@tdcounseling.com

tdcounseling.com

Wesley Harris

Vice President of Plant Engineering, UPS

Wesley is a graduate of Tennessee State University with a bachelor of science degree in electrical engineering. For more than thirty-two years, Wes has helped UPS deliver. He has had various assignments in the company, including operations manager, project engineer, corporate program manager, environmental coordinator, district plant engineering manager, and district labor relations manager. He masterminds plant engineering for the United States.

On the weekends, Wesley serves as the Senior Pastor of The Lord's House International Ministries, a nondenominational group of caring people. He is a past board chair for the Central Florida Urban League and is a past board member of the Edgewood Children's Ranch.

Wesley and his wife, Yvette, have been married for twenty-seven years and they have four wonderful children. Wesley enjoys relaxing with basketball, racquetball, and football.

Connect with Wes:

(407) 405-1061

revwesharris@aol.com

www.thelordshouseintl.org

Scott Humphrey

CEO, World Floor Covering Association

Scott, a graduate of Belmont University in Nashville, Tennessee, spends much of his free time teaching performance skills that inspire people of all ages to grow and prosper. For over twenty years, he has written columns in national publications focused on leadership and life skills.

Prior to his position as CEO of the WFCA, Scott was with Shaw Industries for twenty-five years. His final role there was as the director of Shaw's aligned-dealer network. He was charged with managing all the programs and benefits that serviced 2,100 of Shaw's most loyal retailers. Scott also served Shaw in training, motivating, and recruiting thousands of employees.

Scott and his wife, Tonjua, have four children—triplet daughters and one son. They live in Chatsworth, Georgia.

Connect with Scott:

(706) 217-1183, WFCA

shumphrey@wfca.org

tripletsdad@live.com

wfca.org

www.magneticbuildingsolutions.com

Dr. Jada Jackson

Counselor, Total Life Counseling Center

Emotional Mojo talk-show host Dr. Jada Jackson is known for her transparent, practical style of communicating and teaching. Her ultimate goal is to guide women into meaningful and purposeful living, particularly in the areas of personal enrichment, emotion management, and beauty enhancement.

Dr. Jackson holds a doctorate from Argosy University in Counselor Education and Supervision, a master of science degree in Counseling Psychology with a concentration in mental health from Palm Beach Atlantic University, a master of arts degree in Human Services Counseling, and a bachelor of arts degree in Professional Communication, both from Regent University. She is a Licensed Mental Health Counselor in Florida and a Licensed Professional Counselor in Texas. She is also a National Certified Counselor and a member of the National Board of Certified Counselors.

Before establishing her publishing company, Dr. Jackson began a rewarding career as a commentator and spokesmodel for Ebony Fashion Fair, the world's largest traveling fashion show. An entrepreneur at heart, she owns Jada's Life Development Institute, Jada's Modeling Institute, and Be-You! Foundation, a nonprofit organization. She is the author of Be-You-Tiful, a power-packed, practical application guide to becoming a better you.

Dr. Jackson enjoys speaking to young people and adults across the country, encouraging them to do their best, love themselves, and reach for higher heights. Through her books, speaking, and upcoming multimedia ventures, Jada is impacting the lives of many who are facing the same struggles and pain she has experienced. Jada's passion is to ensure that every life she touches will become more meaningful and more Be-You-Tiful!

Connect with Jada:

(469) 757-5215

jada@totallifecounseling.com

www.jadajackson.com

Ronald Joselin

Founder and CEO, Inspire International

Ronald was born and raised in Chile, and he left with a suitcase of dreams. Ronald is an author, researcher, entrepreneur, and international speaker. An accomplished executive with domestic and international experience, he has traveled the world holding conferences in more than nineteen countries, working on strategic growth for better leaders and professionals in the industry. He is a bilingual (English–Spanish), results-oriented, decisive leader with proven success in new market identification and strategic positioning for multimillion-dollar organizations.

Ronald understands that humanity suffers from three global problems: disease, poverty, and hopelessness. He and his wife, along with a talented team, decided to create a vehicle that will empower people to eradicate these problems in their lives. Their commitment is to focus on the solution, not the problem. Ronald's deepest desire is to inspire more people to have great lives in prosperity and good health and to fulfill their dreams.

He and his wife, Dr. Alexandra, have one son, Ronnie A. They live in Arkansas, and they travel the world helping people.

Connect with Ronald:

(501) 358-4946

rjoselin@inspirewworldwide.com

www.inspireworldwide.com

Aaron Kruse

Founder and CEO, Kingdom Allies Consulting

Aaron Kruse lives a consistent blend of business, ministry, and family. A pastor for ten years, he currently serves as the Director of Campus Development for a growing multisite church with seventeen locations and counting. Aaron oversees and leads a team that is responsible for all new-build and remodel construction projects.

He is the founder of Kingdom Allies Consulting, which exists to help other businesses leverage the tools available in this digital marketing age to measure the right things and get their messages to the right people. He also cofounded and is helping build Emprise Digital, a company that spends every ounce of its time and energy to use Google Grants to grow the vision of churches and nonprofits, giving them access to significant digital marketing power with limited resources.

Aaron has been married to his wife, Angela, for eleven years. They have three children ages five and under, which makes every day an adventure!

Connect with Aaron:

(501) 733-9877

aaron@kingdomallies.com

emprisedigital.co

Jon Langford

Founder, The Gathering INC

Jon is first and foremost a family man. He and his wife, Heather, are both natives of the Atlanta, Georgia area, where they spent the first third of their lives together starting a family. During that time, Jon amassed twenty years of experience as a minister and pastor at Rehoboth Baptist Church in Tucker, Georgia.

In 2011, Jon and Heather relocated to Orlando, Florida with the children to launch a missional community called "The Gathering" that serves the hospitality industry. It has truly been a "family" adventure to the Entertainment Capital of the World. Jon is a bivocational minister working as a professional-development instructor and public speaker, along with Heather, who is instrumental in driving meaningful relationships and changed lives through the ministry of Love on Stage and outreach of The Gathering INC.

While Jon has master's degrees from both Southeastern Baptist Theological Seminary and Liberty Baptist Theological Seminary, Heather is the true brains behind this family of six, with a bachelor of education degree from the University of Georgia. This family truly loves being together and enjoys traveling, reading, entertaining, and bringing dreams to life.

Connect with Jon:

jon@thegatheringinc.org

www.thegatheringinc.org

www.loveonstage.org

Larry Levine

Sales Trainer; Author

Larry is an international best-selling author of *Selling From the Heart* and a co-host of the *Selling From the Heart* podcast. With thirty years of in-the-field sales experience within the B2B technology space, he knows what it takes to be a successful sales professional.

Larry has successfully sold to customers ranging from up-and-down the street accounts to Fortune 500 companies. In the fall of 2013, he became a corporate major account rep for a Japanese OEM in Los Angeles, California, one of the most competitive markets in the United States.

Today, Larry coaches and inspires sales leaders and their teams to do what he did. Since 2015, he has coached sales professionals across the spectrum of tenured reps to new millennials entering the salesforce. Both groups appreciate the practical, relevant, and "street–savvy" nature of his coaching.

In a world full of empty suits, Larry is passionate about helping sales reps succeed by getting valuable before they get visible. He helps sales teams understand the true value they bring to the market. Then he helps them get visible by combining traditional sales techniques with new social selling strategies.

Larry lives in Thousand Oaks, California, where he is actively involved in Kiwanis and other local nonprofits.

Connect with Larry:

(805) 907-5947

Llevine@sellingfromtheheart.net

www.sellingfromtheheart.net

AC Lockyer

Founder, SoftWash Systems

AC is a third-generation service business entrepreneur and the patriarch of the SoftWash cleaning industry. In 1992, he created a new category in exterior cleaning by blending his degree and experience in horticulture and applying it to the cleaning and treating of building exteriors, thereby offering a true alternative to pressure washing.

In 2006, AC fulfilled a lifelong dream of becoming a professional tournament angler and won the Redfish Tour National Championship. He is the visionary drive to the conglomerate of businesses that make up SoftWash Systems. They are equipping individual businesses in five countries and more than 200 co branded SoftWash Systems Authorized companies in 9 Countries, grossing sales in excess of $60 million yearly.

AC is a Christ follower, husband of Karen, and father to two adult children. He and Karen live in central Florida.

Connect with AC:

(855) 763-8669

Ac@softwashsystems.com

www.softwashsystems.com

David Loveless

Pastor to Pastors; Speaker & Consultant; Author & Podcast Host

David has been speaking publicly for more than thirty-five years and has keynoted countless events and even more church services in fifty different counties. David currently is the Pastor of Discipleship & Group Initiatives at First Baptist Church, Orlando. Prior to that, he was the founder and Lead Pastor of Discovery Church Orlando.

David also served on the advisory team of The Leadership Summit, the largest annual leadership gathering in the world. It features the finest teachers and speakers.

In addition to his current role at First Baptist Church Orlando, Florida he devotes part of his time to coaching, consulting, and speaking to teams and churches around the country. He and his wife help church leaders gain a thriving ministry without losing their soul. He has cowritten three books. The most recent is *Nothing to Prove: Find the Satisfaction and Significance You've Been Striving for at the Core of Your True Identity.*

David and his wife, Caron, of forty-one years, have three sons and eight grandchildren. They enjoy life to the fullest just outside Orlando, Florida. In his free time, David enjoys reading, hiking, and kayaking.

Connect with David:

(407) 257-0124

david@davidandcaron.com

www.davidandcaron.com

Pasco Manzo

President and CEO, Teen Challenge New England and New Jersey

Pasco gives oversight to ten long-term residential programs within seven states with insightful leadership skills, creative financial management, and multifaceted administration. He holds annual Leadership Management Conferences and Marriage Retreats, established an "End Addiction" campaign to raise awareness of the drug epidemic in schools, and has promoted several Changing Lives products, including a compilation of a six-book series.

He is the author of *Urim and Thummim—Discovering the Will of God* and *Broken Flowers: A Commentary on the Tragedy of Sex Slavery in America.*

Pasco's studies have earned him a master of arts degree in Christian Ministries and a MDiv Equivalency from Assemblies of God Theological Seminary. He graduated summa and magna cum laude. He has experience as a college adjunct professor and as a public speaker, bringing countless inspirational messages to every populated continent of the world.

Pasco and the wife of his youth, Mary Ann, have three grown children, two daughters-in-law, and six grandchildren. He is passionate about people who need hope. He enjoys travel and the authentic cuisine and culture of his Italian heritage.

Connect with Pasco:

(508) 408-4378

pmanzo@tcnewengland.org

tcnewengland.org

Marc Mero

Founder and CEO, Champion of Choices; Former WWE Wrestling Superstar

Marc experienced his first crisis at age eight, when his parents divorced. He grew up in a single-family home in a poor section of New York, but he wrote down his dreams and goals, setting his sights on athletics. He worked hard to achieve success in hockey, football, boxing, and professional wrestling. After reaching the pinnacle of sports entertainment as a WCW and WWE wrestling champion, Marc suffered enormous loss and learned that money and fame can't buy happiness. He believes that it's not what's in your pocket, it's what's in your heart that truly matters!

Today, Marc selflessly gives of his time and talent to impact young lives with amazing results. Through the nonprofit organization he founded in 2007 called Champion of Choices, this self-proclaimed "Happiest Person on the Planet" shares his powerful story of tragedy and triumph, speaking candidly about where his good and bad choices took him. His anti-bullying, substance-abuse-prevention, and suicide-prevention message reaches students at a heart level during his dynamic stage productions. Lives are saved and changed by Marc's honest portrayal and courage to stand up, step up, and speak up.

Marc lives with his dog, Rocco, in Orlando, Florida.

Connect with Marc:

(407) 862-4800

mark@thinkpoz.org

thinkpoz.org

Mohamid Mobin

Vice President, Citibank (Retired)

Mohamid was educated in Guyana, Canada, and the United States. For most of his career, he worked in the business and computer technology fields, where he held various positions in management.

Over his working career, Mohamid received several awards, including a Corporate Service Excellence Award from his last employer. Based on his prior experience as a police officer, his employer selected him as a first responder to assist at ground zero during the September 11, 2001, Twin Towers attack in New York City. He has also participated in Habitat for Humanity's efforts in building affordable housing in New York City. He received commendation awards for both of these undertakings.

Mohamid is currently retired and living with his wife in Florida. He is the father of two lovely daughters and two outstanding sons, and has five adorable grandchildren.

Connect with Mohamid:

mymobin@gmail.com

Dr. Clarence Nixon

Founder and President, T.LAB

Dr. Nixon is the founder and president of T.LAB, an accelerated learning center for families and students in grades K–12. T.LAB was established to increase the competitiveness of US-based students while leveraging a global leadership model. In FY2012, the Information Technology Senior Management Forum honored Dr. Nixon and T.LAB for the application of technology in education.

In addition, he is the Managing Partner of CNC Group, LLC, a management consulting firm specializing in business transformation, or turnaround management.

Possessing a wide range of management and technology skills, Dr. Nixon is regarded for his general management skills, including marketing, product development, engineering, manufacturing, sales, finance, human resources, and information technology. He was the president and Chief Executive Officer of Real Times, Inc., one of the largest African American newspaper chains in the country.

Building on a strong foundation of an accomplished career within several industries, demonstrating proactive leadership strengths, and perfecting key technological solutions throughout his career, Dr. Nixon is a leading force in change management and the continued emergence of digital technologies.

He holds a PhD in management from Wayne State University, a MSA degree in management from Central Michigan University, and a BS degree in business administration from Upper Iowa University. He has completed executive training from General Electric (Six-Sigma), IBM, Stanford University, The Wharton School of the University of Pennsylvania, Harvard Business School, and multiple other corporate training courses and seminars.

Dr. Nixon is the author of three books: T*he Leadership of Hope*, *From CIO to CEO*, and *Taking the Mountain of Education.*

Connect with Dr. Nixon:

drnixon@gmail.com

tlab-global.com

Paul Perrino

Vice President and Partner, Luxury Meetings Summit; Virtual Health & Fitness Coach

Paul was raised as an Army brat and lived in Texas, Arizona, North Carolina, Panama, and Germany. Although neither of his childhood dreams—being an architect like Mike Brady or the lead singer of a heavy metal band—came to fruition, Paul's big break in the hospitality business came as a boat pilot at Disney's Magic Kingdom.

He has spent his professional career primarily representing luxury hotels for properties such as the Waldorf Astoria Orlando, Walt Disney's Grand Floridian, and The Villas of Grand Cypress. Paul is currently the vice president and business partner of Luxury Meetings Summit, which helps hospitality suppliers and meeting planners connect at more than fifty North American shows annually.

After winning a personal battle with obesity, Paul also owns a virtual health coaching business, through which he helps and motivates others looking to change their lifestyles with the same programs and products that changed his life. He is growing as a presenter and writer, with a focus on inspiring and helping others with personal development.

He and his love, Karen Leigh, enjoy visiting the ocean and anything Starbucks. His two beautiful children, Presley and Nicholas, are avid soccer players, and they relish geeking out with their dad to Star Wars, Marvel, and

Christmas music. Being a University of Florida graduate makes Paul an avid Gators sports fan.

Paul and his family live in central Florida.

Connect with Paul:

(352) 459-6259

pperrino@paulperrino.com

www.PaulPerrino.com

Instagram: @paulperrino

Facebook: @paulperrinoinspires

James Reid (J. R.)

Certified High-Performance Coach

J. R. is an entrepreneur, Certified High-Performance Coach, former Division 1 athlete, and the creator of Championship Families. He is also a proud husband and father of three.

His mission is simple: bring the family back into sports and business. After almost losing his family to the cutthroat nature of specific industries, J. R. has dedicated his life to help champions win at home just as much as in sports and business. From firsthand experience, he knows they can.

High-performance coaching is J. R.'s specialty and passion. Specifically, he helps his individual and organizational clients acquire, refine, and master advanced tools and disciplines proven to accelerate next-level growth and boost clarity, energy, courage, productivity, and influence. Since 2005, J. R. has coached some of the most elite athletes and entrepreneurs in the country, the biggest brands in sports, and several entrepreneurial organizations and start-ups.

His story of family and career restoration has been featured in the book *Your Best Year Ever* and the popular online course, "5 Days to Your Best Year Ever," both by New York Times best-selling author and world-renowned leadership mentor, Michael Hyatt.

J. R. earned his Juris Doctorate and master's degrees in business administration from Louisiana State University, and he holds a bachelor of arts degree in communication from the University of Iowa. He also earned an Executive Certificate in Branding from Northwestern University's Kellogg School of Management.

He lives in Winter Garden, Florida, with his wife, Jessica, their two sons, Caleb and Noah, and their daughter, Madison. When he's not coaching, J. R. finds himself engaged in ongoing personal and professional development, CrossFit training, golfing, spending engaged time with his family, and mentoring young entrepreneurs, students, and athletes.

Connect with J. R.:

jr@jamesreid.com

jamesreid.com

Roy Reid

Executive Director of Communications, Advent Health System

Roy Reid is a leading authority on public relations, business communications, and marketing and has extensive experience in health care. He works with business leaders as a counselor, strategist, and coach to grow, maintain, and protect their interests. He is the Executive Director of Communications for Advent Health Florida Division.

Formerly, he was at the University of Central Florida College of Business, and prior to that, he was a partner with Consensus Communications, an Orlando, Florida-based public relations firm. He also served as Director of Corporate Communications for the nation's largest hospital, Florida Hospital. In 2013, 2014, 2015, and 2016, the group Trust Across America/ Trust Around the World named Roy as one of the "Top 100 Thought Leaders Influencing Trusted Business Behavior."

Roy is the author of *Outrageous Trust®*, a program that provides a framework and understanding of how to improve results by improving relationships through a more intentional and mindful effort to earn, cultivate, and restore trust.

Roy earned a degree in business administration with a minor in communications from the University of Central Florida, where he served as student body president. He is a Certified Public Relations Counselor of the Florida Public Relations Association.

A student and instructor of martial arts, he holds a fourth-degree black belt in Taekwondo.

Roy and his family live in central Florida.

Connect with Roy:

(407) 694-3533

roy.reid@adventhealth.com

www.adventhealth.com

R. D. Saunders

Vice President of Advancement EQUIP Leadership (Founded by John Maxwell)

Born in central Ohio, R. D. had leadership experiences in music and church ministry. After graduating from Ohio Christian University, he spent twenty-two years in pastoral ministry, leading churches in Ohio, Florida, and Georgia.

In 2002, when R. D. began to serve as an Associate Trainer for John Maxwell's EQUIP Leadership organization, he began to see firsthand the needs of the global community. In 2009, he was called to lead Network of Caring, a charitable organization dedicated to bringing hope and healing to the neediest people in the world. For eight years, he served as the Chief Significance Officer (Executive Director) of Network of Caring, managing operations in numerous world areas. In addition to his duties at Network of Caring, R. D. was the primary speaker for Leading With 20/20 Vision, teaching leadership and personal growth to hundreds of thousands of businesspeople around the world.

Now, as the Director of Advancement for EQUIP Leadership, R. D. works closely with the many churches and businesspeople who fund the global ministry of EQUIP and her founder, Dr. John C. Maxwell. R. D. is a gifted communicator and creative thinker who brings passion and innovation to all he does.

He has two sons and lives with his wife, Shelli, in Buford, Georgia.

Connect with RD:

rd.sainders@equip.org

maxwellcenter.compartner/equip

Dr. Amber Selking

Performance Consultant; Director of People Performance, Lippert Components, Inc.

As a former soccer player at the University of Notre Dame, where she graduated with a Management Consulting degree, Amber started her career in human resources with a global manufacturing company. After recognizing a similar performance dynamic in business as she experienced in sports, she returned to graduate school to better understand the art and science of human high performance. She earned a PhD in Applied Sport & Performance Psychology from the University of Missouri and a master's degree in Sport & Performance Psychology from the University of Denver.

Dr. Selking founded the Selking Performance Group, whose mission is to help individuals, sports teams, and business organizations unleash performance excellence by tapping into the power of mindset and leadership. She speaks to organizations around the world and serves as the mental performance consultant to Head Coach Brian Kelly and the Notre Dame Football team. She has also served as an adjunct professor in the business school at Notre Dame.

In 2018, she joined Lippert Components, Inc., a publicly traded, global manufacturing company headquartered in Elkhart, Indiana as their Director of People Performance. She oversees the culture and people-development initiatives for the organization and works to drive team member engagement at every layer of the business. Combined, her expertise is in optimizing human performance by teaching people about how their brains work, providing strategies to build mindsets that facilitate success, and partnering with leaders to build people systems that are most conducive to high performance.

Dr. Selking also hosts a podcast called *Building Championship Mindsets*, which has more than 100k downloads and has been used in Johannesburg, South Africa, to build productive mindsets in young people.

She grew up raising livestock in a small town in northeastern Pennsylvania. Now she lives in South Bend, Indiana with her husband, Aaron, and their Doberman Pinscher, Rockne.

Connect with Dr. Selking:

(352) 989-2127

amber@selkingperformance.com

selkingperformance.com

www.lci1.com

Dr. Mike Smalley

Minister; Founder, Mike Smalley Ministries

Dr. Smalley is one of America's most dynamic and sought-after speakers. He preached his first sermon at fourteen years old, pastored a church at twenty-four, and engaged in full-time evangelistic ministry at age thirty.

Since then, Dr. Smalley has helped plant sixty-four churches internationally, including some in Africa and Central America, and he has spoken to more than 4,000 audiences in thirty-three nations. He has appeared on numerous television and online shows and national radio programs, and he is the author of ten books. Dr. Smalley is passionate about honoring people, locking arms with them, and helping them achieve the dreams God has given them.

He has three children and lives in Dallas, Texas.

Connect with Dr. Smalley:

(214) 334-9932

msmalley66@gmail.com

mikesmalley.com

Dr. Paul C. Sorchy II

Founder and CEO, Life Center; Chiropractor

Dr. Paul Sorchy is a Florida native from Tarpon Springs. In 1995, he graduated from Life University with his doctorate in chiropractic. He opened his practice for business in Florida in 1998 and is a continued member of the Chamber of Commerce. He earned a prestigious fellowship in Chiropractic Biophysics, an advanced chiropractic technique, in 2004. He is also certified in physical therapeutics and several other techniques or forms of adjusting.

In 1998, the Florida Chiropractic Society named Dr. Paul as New Chiropractor of the Year. In 2003, the National Congressional Commission's Physician's Advisory Board named him Physician of the Year. He was a co-chairman on that board in 2002.

Dr. Paul has worked as a personal consultant for a chiropractic consulting group. He is the president of America's first for-profit Christian gym franchise, Lord's Gym. He has appeared on FOX News and CNN; has been featured in Men's Fitness magazine, and is ordained through Lion's Roar International as a marketplace minister. His chiropractic practice and gym are in Clermont, Florida. He is committed to helping people being fully alive by being fully healthy.

He and his wife, Julie, live in Winter Garden, Florida. They are the proud parents of a son, Paulie, and a daughter, Jocelyn.

Connect with Dr. Paul:

(352) 394-7577

drsorchy@icloud.com

clermontspine.com

Terry Steen

Regional VP and Consultant, AG Financial Solutions; Cofounder, Fearless Faith Ministries

Terry was raised in Iowa and grew up loving God, his church, sports, and music. After earning his accounting degree and MBA, he devoted forty years to assisting nonprofit ministries and the local church.

He has served in various leadership roles, including CFO, Executive Pastor, adjunct university professor, and workshop and public speaker.

Currently, Terry serves as a church consultant with AG Financial Solutions, assisting churches and pastors in the area of finance and acquiring funds for ministry. He is also a cofounder of a social media ministry called Fearless Faith Ministries. It was created to pray for, inspire, and encourage people to live a fearless life through faith in God.

You can receive your daily "Morning Cup of Inspiration" devotion at www.facebook.comFFM60.

Terry lives in Tampa, Florida with his beautiful wife, Karen. He has one incredible daughter, a son-in-law, and three priceless grandchildren. He loves them even more than Dippin' Dots and Lucky Charms cereal.

Connect with Terry:

(417) 848-6755

twsteen007@gmail.com

www.ffaith.org

www.agfinancial.org

Bradley Stroud

President and CEO, StroudLink

After graduating from college and spending more than fifteen years of ministry work in two of the largest religious organization in the nation, Bradley felt led to move into the business community. In 1997, he started working in a unique industry known as Professional Employer Organizations (better known as PEOs). He worked for three of the top PEO firms in the country, creating the knowledge base to serve businesses and understand the industry.

In 2004, after realizing there was a tremendous demand to help businesses reduce labor costs, remove liabilities, and create better efficiencies, Bradley established StroudLink, a PEO brokerage service. StroudLink represents many of the top PEO services nationwide. Given the fact that every business is different and unique, StroudLink was designed specifically to help businesses find the right PEO service that best fits their own specific challenges and goals.

He is blessed with three successful children (Zach, Amanda, and Joshua) and seven perfect grandchildren (Dayton, Dillon, Porter, Gauge, Addison, Harley, and Ryker).

Bradley lives in San Antonio, Texas.

Connect with Bradley:

(210) 877-2148

bradley@stroudlink.com

www.stroudlink.com

Duncan Wardle

Former Head of Innovation and Creativity, Disney; Founder, iD8 & innov8

Duncan led the innovation team that helped Imagineering, Lucasfilm, Marvel, Pixar, and Disney Parks innovate, creating magical new storylines and experiences for consumers around the globe. As founder of iD8 & innov8, he now brings his extensive Disney experience as an Innovation Speaker, delivering keynotes, workshops, and ideation forums around the globe. His focus is helping companies embed a culture of innovation into everyone's DNA.

With an infectious energy and playful collaboration, Duncan pushes executives and their teams to overcome preconceived ideas, act more audaciously, and develop their own innovation "light switch," which is a method to activate the creative parts of their brains and access the ideas that turn ordinary companies into industry leaders.

Connect with Duncan:

duncanjwardle@gmail.com

duncanwardle.com

David W. Welday III

President, HigherLife Publishing

David is an accomplished out-of-the-box thinker, gifted communicator, high-energy motivator, trainer, marketing strategist, publisher, and coach. Whether working with a client one-on-one or speaking to a packed house, David is known for his passionate, high-energy, and infectious demeanor and presentation. David is president of HigherLife Publishing and Marketing, Inc. (www.ahigherlife.com) and Executive Director of Next

Generation Institute (www.nexgeninstitute.com). He also manages the publishing imprints for The Savage Group (www.johnsavage.com) and The Billion Soul Network (www.billion.tv).

David has served in the publishing and marketing world for more than thirty years and has delivered 500+ percent growth for nationwide periodicals, developed *New York Times* bestselling authors, and created award-winning curriculum resources. In addition, he is a Certified Professional Coach and is an Energy Leadership Index Master Practitioner with the Institute for Professional Excellence in Coaching.

David has been married to his lovely wife, Amy, for more than forty years, and they live in Oviedo, Florida. They have three grown sons, three wonderful daughters-in-law, and a growing number of grandchildren.

Connect with David:

(407) 563-4806

dwelday@ahigherlife.com

www.ahigherlife.com

Dan Wheeler

President, Fearless Faith Ministries; Former Senior QVC, Host

During the spring semester of 1974, Dan hosted his first radio show on his college campus station in Springfield, Missouri. That was his first taste of "live broadcasting." Forty-four years later, Dan has logged more than eleven thousand hours of live television. That's more than Jay Leno and David Letterman combined.

For twenty-nine years, Dan was one of the top hosts for QVC, the number one electronic retailer in the world. He has interviewed hundreds of superstars from the world of sports, entertainment, politics, and industry. His long list of interviews includes Joe DiMaggio, Mickey Mantle, Cal Ripken, Jr., George Foreman, Magic Johnson, Joe Montana, Dan Marino, Bob Hope, Charlton Heston, Smokey Robinson, Willie Nelson, Darryl Hall, and John Oates, along with many others.

In 1999, Dan wrote a book entitled *Best Seat in the House*, in which he chronicled many untold stories of sports legends such as Joe DiMaggio, Mickey Mantle, and George Foreman.

In 2015, Dan's wife of thirty-one years passed into eternity after a three-year battle with stage IV cancer. He saw many powerful examples of God's love and grace during that time and recently released his second book, *Hurricane of Love: My Journey with Beth Wheeler*.

Dan retired from QVC at the end of 2017 after twenty-nine years to pursue full-time ministry. In 2016, he formed Fearless Faith Ministries with two college friends. They currently produce short, inspirational messages every day on their Facebook page, @FFM60.

Dan currently lives in Coatesville, Pennsylvania with his dog, Zoey. He has two daughters and three very special, perfect grandchildren.

Connect with Dan:

(610) 733-6949
Dwheels222@gmail.com
www.fearlessfaithministries.org

IF YOU'RE A FAN OF THIS BOOK, HELP SPREAD THE WORD ABOUT WOW!

So, hopefully you were WOWed by reading through this book...and you are now an official WOW Factor FAN. We refer to you as a fellow WOWZER. We know, kind of silly, but hey, we love to define words right?

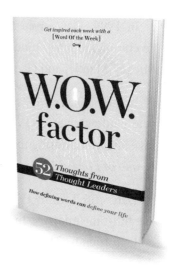

So, what is a Wowzer??? He or she is someone who loves to discover new meanings of words – not just any word, but words that motivate and inspire. WOWZERS get excited when they dig up some awesome truth that pulls them into becoming a better person, a better spouse, a better employer or employee, a better version of themselves!

A WOWZER is one who cares so much for others they can't hold these discoveries just to themselves – after all, they are a part of the WOW fctor movement!

WILL YOU HELP US SPREAD THE WORD?

There are several ways you can help us get the word out about the message of this book…

- Post a 5-Star review on Amazon.

- Write about the book on your Facebook, Twitter, Instagram – any social media you regularly use!

- If you blog, consider referencing the book, or publishing an excerpt from the book with a link back to www.wowfactor.live. You have our permission to do this as long as you provide proper credit and backlinks.

- Recommend the book to friends – word-of-mouth is still the most effective form of advertising.

- You can order more WOW Factor books from AMAZON & Barnes & Noble or where ever you purchase your favorite books. You can also order direct from: www.wowfactor.live

amazon   **BARNES&NOBLE**

WHAT WORD HAS INSPIRED YOU?

Perhaps there's a word that has inspired you. We are already connecting with gifted leaders to contribute to the next volume of WOW Factor. If you would like to be considered as a contributing writer, please reach out to us. We will share with you the details you need to know.

Contact us at: info@wowfactor.live

NEED A DYNAMIC SPEAKER FOR YOUR NEXT EVENT?

One of the amazing realities about becoming a fellow WOWZER is your connection with each of the thought leaders that helped make this volume a success. Be sure to check out the biographical summaries of all our contributing writers. If you like what they said, reach out and invite them to speak at your next event and find out what other resources and training they have to offer.

If you have any questions about the movement, want to get pricing on some bulk copies, or have a questions that you just need to know, reach out to info@wowfactor.live

Chris Gingrasso, the founder of the WOW Movement, is a dynamic sales trainer and speaker and is available to bring a new level of energy, insight and impact to your next event. To connect with Chris, contact us at: info@wowfactor.live

Facebook: WOW Factor Movement

Instagram: @wow_factor_movement

Twitter: @wow_movement

LinkedIn: @Chris Gingrasso